David Scott.

D1477284

Sailing Craft
of the
British Isles

Sailing Craft
of the
British Isles

ROGER FINCH

with illustrations by the author

Collins

William Collins Sons & Co Ltd
London · Glasgow · Sydney · Auckland
Toronto · Johannesburg

First published 1976
© Inge Moore and Roger Finch 1976

ISBN 0 00 219710 3

Made and printed in Great Britain by
Jolly and Barber Ltd
Rugby, Warwickshire

Contents

Acknowledgments

For their assistance and advice in the preparation of this book the author would particularly like to thank James and Inge Moore, whose idea it originally was, and Marjorie Smith for her tireless help in the preparation of the manuscript. There has been as well the ungrudging help of innumerable retired seafaring gentlemen, longshoremen and fishermen who, over the past forty years and from places as far apart as North Uist and South Devon have given freely of their time to recall the days that are gone and the ways of sail and oar.

Sailing Craft of Great Britain

Now that the sailing craft of Britain have gone we realise that we have lost something precious. The sailing vessel is a beautiful thing, whether at rest or at sea, but with its passing has gone a way of life as well. It was a way of life beset with hardship and danger, ill rewarded and leaving little profit in many cases beyond which it was possible to support more than a poverty-stricken existence. Yet the skill and hardihood which it demanded deserve our respect and understanding and the variety of the build and rig of the craft that were used was of an astonishing individuality. Each beach, harbour and creek around our coast developed its own particular type, its form and rig, its sails and fishing gear, shaped by experience and honed by use over the centuries. The craft were unembellished and there was rarely any substantial margin of profit available for expending upon decoration. Indeed it is their structural soundness for their purpose, within the limitation of the materials and technique available, that is perhaps the core of their appeal and makes their study and recording worth while.

It would be wrong to over-sentimentalise the appeal of the traditionally-built and designed wooden sailing vessels, any more than one should be nostalgic over the grimly demanding existence that those who sailed them experienced. Whole communities could find themselves bereft of a quarter of their menfolk as the result of a single unheralded storm. It is to the growing awareness by a wide public of this situation that some of our first accurate information of early fishing craft depends and of the conditions under which they worked. With a commendable energy and thoroughness the Victorians commissioned an enquiry into the tragic losses amongst the Scottish fishing fleet. The report was published, with plans of vessels and harbours, in 1849, and perhaps its most telling comment was that the craft were almost all inadequate for the work they were intended to perform and that the high reputation that some vessels had was due to the skill and dexterity of their crews rather than any inherent qualities in the boats. But great strides were made in the development of all the sailing craft of our islands in the succeeding fifty years; they became safer, more weatherly and speedier so that in the decade immediately prior to the First World War there was a trimness and overwhelming presence about them and a robust individuality which is immediately appealing. Nevertheless, fishing and trading under sail remained until its end a dangerous and demanding occupation.

The point of development that was reached just before the introduction of the marine internal combustion engine changed a whole way of life was the result of changes that had progressed slowly, but with ever greater speed and a growing tendency to specialisation, over the centuries. It left in its wake places which were – for reasons of remoteness, a lack

The mule-rigged spritsail barge *Scotia*, built in 1903 by Everard at Greenhithe on the Thames. She traded coastwise and was eventually lost off Yarmouth. (National Maritime Museum)

of raw material or sheer poverty – still using techniques and preserving ancient ways long since abandoned in ports and on coasts which were more fortunately placed. Change came, but only slowly. There were exceptions to this, such as at Polperro where a gale in 1891 swept into the tiny harbour such huge seas that the fishing fleet was almost obliterated. As a result a re-building took place and a radically different sail plan was adopted by the fishermen when they ordered their new boats. At Grimsby in the eighteen seventies, in less than a decade, a town of fishermen and a port for hundreds of magnificently powerful sailing trawlers grew up on a marsh beside the Humber. For the rest, new hull forms, different styles of rig and new fishing techniques were viewed with suspicion. Unsuccessful experimentation was paid for at sea by not only a lost investment but lost lives. So it is not surprising to find preserved in remoter ports of our coastline, even in a few cases to this day, every stage of development in the evolution of the sailing fishing and trading craft.

To further our understanding of what may appear to the uninitiated a list of quaint and confusing names, we may divide the wide range of sailing craft into occupational categories. Humblest of all, requiring the most modest accumulation of capital to build, were the longshore boats. While it is a constant source of surprise to learn what voyages were made in the most unassuming craft, these, as the name implies, were usually open boats launched from beaches and working within a few miles of the shore. Decked fishing craft were often not much larger than the biggest longshore boats but by reason of their deep keels and seagoing rig had a much wider range of action. They were concentrated in harbours and rapidly developed in response to economic and technological changes ashore. The tonnage of shipping coming from overseas increased a hundredfold during the nineteenth century and the pilots that served them used craft of an especial quality. The element of competition intrinsic in the pilotage system produced vessels which had a

One of E. & J. Goldsmith's steel coasting barges running up Channel. She is setting a squaresail, boomed out to windward to help balance the mainsail and ease the task of the helmsman at the wheel. (Noakes)

The mate of the last commercial sailing barge *Cambria* stands by the main brail winch which will gather up the mainsail. (Author)

quality and variety unusual in traditional craft. On the fringes of the pilotage system were the hovellers. These too were boats developed to a fine degree by the competition to which their owners were subjected. The hovellers were parasitic upon the unfortunate amongst the great fleets of sailing ships which the nineteenth century saw accumulate in times of bad weather and continuing foul winds at certain well known roadsteads and safe anchorages along the coast. The hovellers took out pilots and replaced lost and damaged ground tackle: they supplied food and extra hands when the regular crews of the beleaguered ships were too exhausted to battle on any longer. Salvaging lost cargoes and wrecked vessels was all part of their work and their craft were consequently built to withstand hard usage and to carry heavy loads. The crews were viewed with understandable suspicion by their contemporaries – as are all who make a livelihood ultimately derived from the misfortunes of others. But before the day when the lifeboat service became securely established many a seaman owed his life to the hovellers' skill and daring.

The trading craft of the last days of sail were divided into two groups. There were those that worked about the rivers and estuaries, with their crews, as it were, keeping one leg on dry land and in some cases, in defiance of seafaring traditions, a bicycle on the mainhatch; for a day's trading would perhaps take them no further from their home port than a few miles and who would prefer the tiny dark forecastle in the evening to home and the pub? On the other hand were schooners and ketches who could, and still occasionally did, go deepsea, but had for the most part been relegated to coasting as the trades which once provided cargoes that took them to Newfoundland, South America and the Mediterranean ceased to exist. Between these two extremes were vessels which were evolved to sail inland to farm quays or industrial backwaters and yet could cope with the Narrow Seas and the weather such voyaging could bring. It was the life experienced aboard these vessels, alone perhaps of all those that were spent by men who sailed for a living, that may justifiably excite in us today a modest envy. Until, that is, we recall that unloading the cargo, usually by turning the handles of a primitive dolly winch from seven in the morning until six in the evening, was an accepted part of the crew's duties.

There was, in all truth, a less hard and fast division than in retrospect we tend to impose upon such a rich pattern of craft and sail. Colne smacks, built for fishing, would load new potatoes in Jersey and bring them home to Essex. Beach-boats would go trawling although the sail-plan they had was ill-adapted for it, and when the introduction of steam-trawlers flooded the market for fishing vessels, many were bought very cheaply and run as cargo carriers lumping coal to little harbours on the East Coast.

Origins

Britain has no Zuider Zee whose draining exposed the remains of the fishing craft and coasters stretching back over five centuries. Perhaps the water-level of a Scottish loch may retreat to expose the dugout canoes which were surprisingly in use as late as Elizabethan times. Chance discoveries by industrial development may very occasionally uncover the barely recognisable bones of a medieval trader, but these are little upon which to build an authentic picture of our earliest fishing and river craft. The coracles of Wales and the Welsh border still in use, perhaps provide a clue to how man first got himself afloat while the curraghs of the West Coast of Ireland show this simple technique for boat-building developed to its limit. It has survived there because of the shortage of sizeable native timber and an economy which until recently has been very limited in resources. On the shores of East Anglia and until recently in the Shetlands the simple double-ended open boat, clench-built from wide planks, probably preserves the appearance of the longshoreman's boat before the introduction of more sophisticated building methods in the eighteenth century. These new methods percolated down to influence vernacular boat-building only slowly. It is important to recall that fishing was already subject to new techniques introduced to make the pursuit of an increasingly wasting asset less difficult. When the finest fish could be caught by hook and line immediately off our shores, and for a smaller market, there was no need for large decked vessels scouring the sea bottom with trawls.

The preservation of herring by a variety of saltings, packings, smokings and dryings was initiated on a commercial scale by the Hollanders. It was said of the North Sea that 'it was the principal gold-mine of the Dutch' and their fleet of 2,000 vessels worked their way down from Shetland to the Straits of Dover throughout the eighteenth century and earlier. We attempted to imitate them with a similar large-scale organisation of fishing busses, accompanied by fast sailing auxiliary craft to ferry the catch ashore and bring supplies, as well as Naval vessels to provide protection, but this never amounted to anything comparable to Holland's 'nation afloat'. Plans of these wooden British factory-ships survived, published in F. H. Chapman's magnificent book of ship plans, which first appeared in 1768. They show a wall-sided, double-ended vessel, over 60 ft. in length and of 77 tons burden. There is little in the design of its hull to distinguish it from the smaller contemporary trading craft. The triangular mizzen sail, used when they were riding to their nets and the conical capstan on deck for hauling the warps in are the principal differences, for the square mainsail and topsail were not unusual in small traders in the eighteenth century. But the busses were the aristocrats among the fishing fleets. For the rest, open boats of varying sizes predominated. The specialisation of fishing craft in particular did not occur

The smaller class of Essex fishing smacks set summer sails for a regatta on the Blackwater.

The Essex cutter smack *Dove*, built at Brightlingsea; projecting from the counter can be seen the iron head of the fish trawl. (J. H. Clegg)

until the increasing improvement of communications on land could provide wider and more lucrative markets for a variety of catches. One type of offshore boat had to serve many purposes. Primarily it had to provide accommodation for the bulky mass of sodden drift-nets and, hopefully, an equally bulky catch of wet fish. Only reluctantly were boats decked and hatches provided.

The end of the Napoleonic Wars saw an expansion of the herring fishery now that the seas were free from privateers and from Naval vessels seeking to impress seamen from fishing boats and carry them off to a life of brutality aboard a man-of-war. Harbours were expanded or built where there had previously been nothing but open beaches, particularly on the North East Coast of Scotland and the South West Peninsula. This enabled deeper draught boats to be built, their size no longer restricted by their having to be dragged ashore when fishing was done. There emerged the form of fishing vessels which are recognisably like those depicted in the second section of the book. Improved weaving by machinery produced a better quality of sail cloth, better able to hold its shape and longer lasting. Cotton canvas augmented the heavier flax. This indirectly had a far-reaching effect upon the sail-plan of vessels. The simply-cut square-sail and its relation the lug had the advantages of simplicity, but set badly when a vessel was close-hauled, doing its best to make the most of a wind dead ahead. A long, light spar known to fishermen as a 'vargord' had been used to extend the weather-leach of a square-sail since Viking times (see Beer Lugger, p. 132) and it seems unlikely that it had ever passed out of use despite there remaining little pictorial evidence of it. It survived, until the introduction of better sailcloth and more effective sail-making in the mid-nineteenth century made its use unnecessary on the majority of boats. Three masts, each lug-rigged, were the most common rig for the big herring drifters and there is ample pictorial evidence for their appearance as husky, sea-kindly craft in the paintings of the Norwich School and the engravings of E. W. Cooke. A distinctive feature of these earlier luggers was the heavy wooden gallows aft, into which the mainmast was lowered when riding to the nets. No doubt the heavy hulls needed all the sail they could muster to lug them through a heavy sea and the mainmast was only abandoned with reluctance to make more deck space available.

The fore and aft rig developed rapidly for use aboard both fishing and small trading vessels at the beginning of the nineteenth century. It was relatively economical in men, spars and cordage, enabled a vessel to work well to windward and it had the advantage of providing a powerful tow which could be nicely adjusted to the use of the beam trawl then coming into use. A vessel could so employ its sails as to lose speed and lie-to, riding the waves without forward movement and in comparative safety – an essential requirement when fishing gear needed adjustment and repair and the catch stowed below; far from port a storm could be safely ridden-out in this way. The lugsail, primitive as it was, nevertheless proved a long time a-dying. The improvement of a sailing vessel's rig was usually made in response to the necessity for economies in the number of the crew. Aboard a herring lugger a crew of five or six was always necessary to handle the nets and clear them of fish so that huge sails such as the Scottish luggers adhered to could be handled on a fishing boat which would have rapidly got out of control aboard a trading craft with its small crew. By the end of the era many fishing craft were fitted with auxiliary steam engines for hauling the nets and these could also be used for handling the sails. When one queries an apparent anachronism in the shape of a vessel or the style of the rig, why a hull seems to have a form which disappeared elsewhere in the eighteenth century, a reason is sure to be found in the especial conditions under which the craft work, the way they use their fishing gear or, if they are trading vessels, load or discharge their cargoes.

Building

The hull-construction of the multiplicity of sailing craft around the British Isles seventy years ago fell into two clearly defined categories. One method, stemming from a Northern European tradition, of which the Vikings were the greatest exponents and rooted in the immense resources of timber available, is known as clench or clinker construction. The other technique is called carvel and possibly originates in the classical world and only reached our shores to make a lasting impact upon ship-building technology as late as the fifteenth century. The clench building tradition was employed in the construction of small vessels in Britain from the Dark Ages onward with surprisingly few modifications and is occasionally used today. If the master-builder responsible for the 80 ft. vessel discovered under a Suffolk tumulus, dating from the seventh century and known as the Sutton Hoo ship, was confronted with a twentieth century Sheringham crabber lying on a Norfolk beach he would, I feel, show little surprise at its construction. However, he would, once the crabber was afloat, show interest in the rudder hung from the sternpost, for this was an innovation which only became common during the fourteenth century.

Clench building has the advantages of simplicity and although it requires a high level of craftsmanship it employs no great degree of calculation. The vessel is constructed from the 'outside inwards' for the skin is formed and only when half completed is it strengthened internally by frames and transverse beams. The work commences by the setting up of the keel on blocks, under cover if possible, and the stem and stern posts are morticed into it at either end. While the processes that then followed varied from one part of the coast to another, for clench building was essentially a vernacular craft, the basic method was common everywhere in Britain. One wooden mould might be set up amidships on the keel and supported either by struts secured to the ground or, if the vessel was built under cover, to battens nailed to the roof beams. The mould was made from boards and was the full-size midship centre section of the craft's hull. Sometimes this would be augmented with two others, one forward and another aft. The same moulds, slightly modified or altered in their position on the keel, would serve for many boats and give a builder his individual stamp.

Then **V**-shaped grooves were cut into either side of the keel and ran up the stem and the sternpost. In these grooves to port and starboard, the first two and the lowest planks of the hull were fitted and were known as the garboard strakes. Then in their turn the other planks were added, each overlapping the one preceding it; the amount of overlap, which was proportionate to the width of the plank, was known as 'lands'. Ageing clench-built craft had quarter-round fillets nailed along the lands to attempt to make good the gaps brought about by hard use and shrinking.

Harwich became known as 'shrimp town' because so many bawleys such as these were owned there. The mate of the bawley has dropped the foresail and jib preparatory to picking up the mooring at the end of a day's fishing. 1893. (Ipswich Libraries)

Each plank was fastened to its neighbour with copper, iron or galvanised nails, clenched or riveted on the inboard over washers known as roves, a job requiring two men, one inboard hammering and another braced against the hull supporting the rivet-head. The boat-builder could employ a minimum of assistants; a pair of sawyers to be employed casually who converted the oak and elm butts seasoning in the shade of the shed to boards and planks; a journeyman to work with chisel and auger while an apprentice held his hammer against the head of the nails as the ends were broken off and riveted over. A boy, to fetch beer, light the stove and be sworn at for not bringing tools quickly enough, completed the work-force of many yards that produced a craft which would serve three generations of fishermen.

To hold the planks of the hull in position while they were riveted together, simple wooden clamps were used or alternatively enormous pegs, similar to old-fashioned clothes' pegs, made from hedgerow timber. As plank by plank the shape of the boat

Two 'convertor smacks' reducing sail as they enter Lowestoft fish dock. Dating from the 1880s, they earned their name from the fact that they could be converted from drift-net fishing to trawling. 1885. (Robert Malster)

unfolded from the keel upward, floors, crossing the keel, were added, but fitted to the already existing shape and not determining it. These floors were shaped or 'joggled' to fit the irregular inner surface of the hull and through-bolted to the keel with long copper bolts or trenails. Trenails were common to all forms of ship-building. They were hardwood pegs which were driven into deep holes made by an auger. Trenails were produced by forcing long lengths of wood, usually stringy oak, through a circular iron collar, fitted with an edged blade. This partly shaped them and partly compressed the fibres. When driven home into the frames they expanded upon immersion in water and held fast. However, it must be admitted that many unidentifiable leaks on wooden vessels have been eventually traced to a defective trenail, or perhaps more accurately a poor shipwright omitting to drive a wedge into the trenail's end to secure it, as good craftsmanship required him to do.

The floors were not fitted with over-much accuracy for this allowed bilge water to run

A clench-built tug tows out a sailing trawler of the Hewett Fleet, originally based at Barking, from Yarmouth Harbour. 1885. (Robert Malster). The brigantine *Mary and Agnes* ashore at Whitby in an autumn gale, 1885. She was built at Sunderland in 1842. Many sailing coasters ended like this, pounded to pieces on a lee shore, unable to weather out a gale. (Sutcliffe Gallery)

A Sheringham crab-boat is carried up the beach by fishermen. (Smiths Suitall, Ipswich)

down to the pump-well. Frames were fitted inside the hull above the floors, sometimes as continuations of them, sometimes slightly aft or forward. Beach-boats had steamed, bent ribs fitted between more substantial sawn frames. An iron or wooden steam chest, which could reduce planks and ribs to a pliable state, was part of a boat-builder's simple equipment. Many clench-built boats had a flat transom, particularly the beach-boats of the South Coast, and this required particular care to plank-up, for the strakes had to be so shaped that they extended to cover a greater area at the stern than the bow. The shell of planking and its frames were finally strengthened with beams, if it was to be decked, or with thwarts for the rowers if it was open. Timber chosen from hedgerow trees, which had grown in distorted shapes, provided naturally grown crooks and curves for breasthooks at the bow, supplied knees to strengthen the stern-post and support the mast-beams and thwarts.

The clench-built hull had distinct advantages for vessels of moderate size that did not habitually carry bulk cargoes and was only slowly replaced in decked craft by carvel building. There are indeed some odd exceptions to the rule that open beach-boats were always clench-built. The little crabbers of North Devon are an example, for they are carvel-built. But clench construction was found almost everywhere along the shores of Britain except for the South West Peninsular. When the writer was first collecting material on sailing craft some forty years ago, the oldest of the fishermen could recall the days when the change from clench to carvel was made.

The bawley boats of the Thames, the oyster smacks of Essex and Kent and the Humber keels were all originally clench-built. There was even a variant of the Thames barge that was constructed in this way and survived into the second half of the nineteenth century while clench-built paddle-tugs worked on the Tyne.

Clench-building had much to commend it. It was cheaper in so far as it did not demand such a wide range of 'compass-timber', the name given to the curved and forked wood that provided the frames for a carvel-built vessel and which became increasingly difficult to obtain. A clench-built boat was more easily repaired and could withstand a great deal of rough treatment due to its inherent pliability; its planks bent before they broke. The boatmen of Hastings, in the days of sail, when landing in a heavy sea, stationed one of their number on the shore with a maul. His task was to rush into the surf in the event of a boat being swamped and to stove in a plank in the bilge of the lugger so that the water

Humber sloops at the entrance of the Hull river on the Humber. The Humber was the meeting place of the keels and the Thames spritsail barges; one of the latter may be seen, dried out, alongside the quay. (Judge)

23

could escape and prevent further catastrophe. The largest clench-built craft were the billy-boys of the Humber: they were up to 70 ft long and carried 120 tons. On the Yarmouth beaches open-boats, the celebrated beach yawls belonging to the salvaging companies, were normally 50 ft. and some as long as 70 ft. overall. Britain's longest lived craft afloat is the Essex oyster smack *Boadicea* of Maldon, built there in 1808. She was originally clench-built, although rebuilt carvel fashion about eighty years later. At the time of her reconstruction evidence of her original appearance was left, for several joggled frames remained in her hull. It was said of the *Boadicea*, as of other craft, that the uneven surface of the clench-built hull gave more lift to the bows and produced a drier ship, for less water came on deck. It was probably not so much any inherent disadvantages that brought about a change to carvel building on larger craft, as the difficulty of handling a trawl over the sides; and when crowded into a harbour clench-built boats grinding together made bad bed-fellows.

Carvel construction involves considerably more draughtsmanship and preparation than the 'chalk line and a good eye' approach of the boat-builder. It requires that once the

A painting by R. Chappell of Goole of the Humber keel *Willie* of Driffield. Chappell was one of the many 'pier-head artists' to whom the seamen turned when they required a colourful and accurate painting of their craft. 1900. (National Maritime Museum)

24

A big herring coble lies ashore at Whitby, 'the haven under hill'. (Sutcliffe Gallery)

keel, with its stem piece and stern post are set up, a series of frames is attached vertically to the keel. Over this rigid skeleton of wood the skin of planks is attached and then reinforced with an inner skin referred to as a ceiling. The frames are each fabricated from a number of pieces and their exact curvature carefully determined before setting up on the keel. Draughting these out, as the naval architect does is a complex task, and was avoided by using models. Where these models survive today, they are our few real source of accurate knowledge of how the hulls of many of our native sailing craft appeared. Unfortunately they are comparatively rare. Until recently their historic value was not appreciated and, unlike the naive paintings by pier-head artists, they were unappreciated as domestic decoration once their immediate purpose was over. It is also certain that the destruction of half-models was carried out by the shipwrights who carved them and who were suspicious that their hard-won knowledge would pass into the hands of their competitors. The appearance of a half-model is certainly perplexing to the un-initiated. It is, as the name implies, a hull model, usually to the scale of one quarter or one half of an inch to one foot, of which usually only the hull's starboard side appears, fixed to a flat board. It is in horizontal laminations, relating to the scale, so that once carved, the model could be taken apart easily. By taking measurements at prescribed intervals across each lamination, vertical sections of the hull could be drawn and then scaled up to full size on the mould-loft floor. This was a floor in the ship-yard covered in blackened canvas and upon which chalked outlines could be drawn. Once the outlines were established then wooden planks would be cut and nailed together to give the outline of a frame; this was then duplicated in the actual scantling that the size of hull required. Hulls were sometimes built with the frames set up amidships at first and then progressing forward and aft. Sometimes the first frames were set up at the stern and work proceeded forward.

Carvel building was a complicated and lengthy process and I must inevitably omit some of its detail. The essentials were, once the frames were in position, for a shipwright to ensure with the help of his adze that there was a fair surface to allow for the covering skin of planking to be fastened without any major irregularities. Each plank was abutted to its neighbour without an attempt to obtain a perfect joint. To ensure a water-tight hull caulking, as hemp unravelled from old rope was known, was forced into the joint by a

In the herring season Whitby's own fishing fleet was augmented by many Scottish herring luggers. Here two are drying their nets, hoisted aloft on booms between the masts. In the foreground are two of the local cobles. (Sutcliffe Gallery)

The ketch *Cantick Head* ashore in Peterhead Harbour 1937. She was built as one of the largest fishing 'zulus' and converted to become a trading vessel, owned in the Orkneys, when steam replaced sail. (Author)

caulking-iron struck by a wooden mallet. The sound of the caulkers at work provided a constant background music in the old shipyard for each mallet struck its own note. The caulkers were preceded by shipwrights, whose dull thudding as they faired up the surface of the planks with their adzes, echoed in the empty wooden hull. There was then iron strapping to be added, deck- planking to be laid, windlass bitts to be set up and hatch-coamings to be fitted. A prosperous owner would commission an appropriate figurehead for the stem-head and the carver would add name and port of registry to the stern. Sometimes a vessel would be launched fully rigged and equipped down to the cups and saucers in the cabin. If trade was brisk and the berth was required for the keel of another

A Loch Fyne herring skiff's crew; a photo taken in Campbeltown Harbour in 1885. (William Anderson)

vessel to be laid immediately, rigging and masting would take place after the vessel had left the ways. In either case it was an occasion for celebration – with beer and goodwill flowing in equal proportions for all involved.

A shipyard which built vessels in the way outlined above required a labour-force much larger and with a wider range of skills than those commanded by the boat-builder and his little band. At least a dozen and sometimes as many as fifty were employed by the yards which built the ketches, schooners and smacks. Most yards had a blacksmith's shop commanded by a traditionally gruff smith, for his workshop could easily become a refuge in cold and wet weather for apprentices, although his hearth was usually surrounded by their tea-cans and potatoes well before dinner time.

A group of workmen at G. & T. Smith's shipyard, Rye, about 1895. Each holds the tool of his craft, adze, saw and maul while the loft-worker holds a wooden mould. Behind rise the frames of a wooden trawler. (Rye Museums)

Few shipbuilders made a fortune. A great deal of money was involved in maintaining a stock of first-class timber and orders were usually paid for by instalments. Vessels were built to a special survey, to secure a classification by Lloyds and this could mean that timber already built into a vessel might have to be removed at considerable trouble and expense. Shipyards made more profit from repairs and the bringing up of vessels on to their slipways for them to be surveyed periodically. Wooden vessels required constant attention. The causes of rot were not fully understood and the traditional methods of building did not allow ventilation nor the easy replacement of components that were diseased. Many shipyards, long after they had launched their last wooden sailing vessel, continued for years servicing those that remained, continuing to use the traditional ways associated with the adze and caulking mallet.

Fishing Ways

The seas of Britain abounded with fish. Their ruthless exploitation over the last half century has so reduced stocks that all fishing is now bringing fewer returns for greater effort and some traditional catches have completely disappeared. The relative inefficiency of the old methods in the days of sail did at least ensure that stocks were only

The Bristol Channel trading smack *Matilda* preparing to unload a cargo from a creek of the river Parrett in Somerset. The *Matilda* was built in 1830 at Bridgwater. (N.P.A.)

The Severn trow *Mary* lying at Dunball Pill in the Bridgwater river. She has the open hold of her type, without hatch covers, and was built at Ironbridge in 1819. (N.P.A.)

very slowly eroded. Nevertheless, the development of the trawl in the mid-nineteenth century was probably stimulated by the catches becoming slowly reduced by the older methods of which lining was the principal technique.

Lining was a fishing method with wide application. Little open boats which might put their baited lines within a mile or less of the shore, yawls working on the edge of the Dogger and great cod-boats 80 ft. or more long and going as far afield as the Faroes, all used a similar technique. Deepsea boats would shoot four or five miles of line with 4,000 hooks while the inshore man would be content with a few hundred yards. Having put down the line the boat then anchored or returned to port, later to return and retrieve the lines which were buoyed to assist recovery. Procuring bait for the hooks was always a problem. Women and children scoured the rocks and pools, and whelks, a much sought-after bait for it stays on the hook well, were captured in baited lures. At sea the yawls carried a boat on deck for netting small herring; the fresher the bait was, the better. Sometimes individual lines were used for cod, turbot and hake. The men fished from the deck with lead sinkers and usually three hooks on each line. If the vessel were fitted with a wet well, a section of the hull amidships made watertight by bulkheads and in which

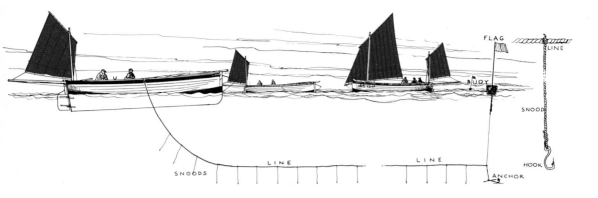

Long lining

sea-water circulated, gaining access by lead pipes, fish could be stored in them alive. When landed on deck, the swim-bladder of the cod was punctured to prevent it 'sounding' and lowered into the wet-well. Upon reaching port they were removed, either for immediate sale or for storage in floating fish-boxes. Before the days of refrigeration and when the supply of ice was both limited and expensive, this was one of the few methods available to ensure a regular supply of fresh fish.

The long liners and the trawlers fished the same waters and the two methods were incompatible. In the end trawling won. Long-lining survived only for catching certain species of fish in shoal or rocky waters where the use of nets would lead to nothing but the loss of gear. The dragging of a net along the smooth stretches of the bottom of the sea had long been a familiar idea before its rapid nineteenth century development into the beam trawl. To drag a heavy frame and attendant net along even the smoothest part of the sea bed meant a loss of all but a fraction of sailing speed. Unless a strong tide could be made to help, such as that in the Bristol Channel or Thames Estuary, it was necessary to work up a sailing speed of eight knots to approach one and a half knots over the ground. Anything less is useless; a reduction in the width of the frame defeated the object of the drag in search of demersal fish. Trawling had to await the development of vessels powerful enough to provide the speed and working facilities and within a price the fishermen could afford. This seems to have occurred in the second quarter of the eighteenth century.

The development of trawls and trawlers is variously claimed by Brixham in Devon and Barking on the Thames. It is perhaps a surprise to learn that Barking, now an industrial suburb of London, with a grimy backwater, was once an independent fishing town on a salty creek surrounded by red-tiled cottages. It flourished as a little port until defeated by pollution and its fishing fleet migrated, with few regrets one may imagine, to Yarmouth in the eighteen fifties. It is certain that there were smacks based there using trawls in 1750, for the unlimited market of nearby London, only a tide from Barking, could absorb all the fish that were caught.

Brixham, the other pioneer, became a trawling port by 1770 at the latest. The Barking men always used an iron trawl head in the shape of a stirrup; the pattern adopted by the Devon fleet and all its offshoots had the side profile of a shoe which seems to indicate independent development. It is more than possible that both were developed from a Dutch original. These iron heads were proportioned to the size of the boats that carried them, but the largest stood four feet high and between their upper rim fixed the great

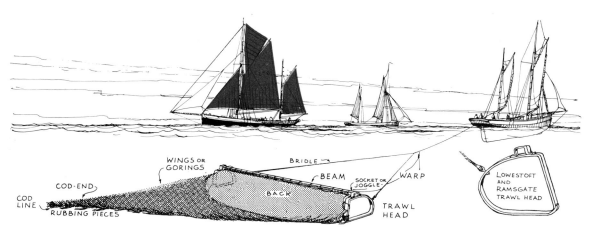

Trawling

wooden trawl beam to which was seized the net and was anything between 36 and 50 ft. in length. While fish swim everywhere only certain areas were suitable for trawling under sail; smacks needed a really fresh breeze in which to work, without too heavy a swell to strain the tackle. A strong wind was essential, but the difference between that and a dangerous gale was hard to anticipate, particularly as the trawl, once shot, would take two to three hours before all could be secured again on deck. The replacement of the handspike windlass by the introduction of the vertical capstan, followed by the installation of the steam winch in the last quarter of the nineteenth century, was an immense relief to trawler-men. The time taken in recovering the nets was reduced by more than half and bigger and more heavy gear could be carried.

These improvements required bigger vessels. The ketch, or, as it was known to the fishermen, dandy rig, was adopted to produce a more easily managed sail-plan aboard smacks, now 70 to 80 ft. overall. Owners were encouraged to put their older cutters on the shipyard ways where they were cut in half and a new midship section built in; the resulting smack emerging to be re-rigged as a ketch and capable of carrying a longer beam. The same revolution in technology that made available the steam winches, had spread rail communications to remote areas which had previously sent their catches to London and other centres of population by fast sailing cutters and horse-drawn vans. As the railways established their network the Humber proved to be the finest and most convenient base. The ever-widening markets led to the trawler stations multiplying with ever-growing fleets and the pioneers of Barking and Brixham at first visited and then settled at Rye, Ramsgate, Yarmouth, Grimsby and Scarborough.

Brixham claims to have discovered the Silver Pits, a prolific trawling ground close by the Dogger Bank, in 1840. Working this area was considered dangerous, even by the standards of the fishermen themselves. In winter the shallow water and steep bank along the northern edge causes heavy breaking seas with no pattern to their run. Many trawlers have been simply overwhelmed by huge rogue waves as they attempted to haul their trawl prior to running before a gale. The final development of trawling under sail was to organise the smacks into fleets under the command of an 'admiral' who directed activities by flag signals by day and a system of lights and flares at night. The object was efficiency. On its way to and from port to deliver its catch and then return to the grounds fishing gear on the smack was lying idle. By 'fleeting' steam-powered fish-carriers could meet the concentration of smacks at sea, collect their catch and then steam at full speed to market. It brought

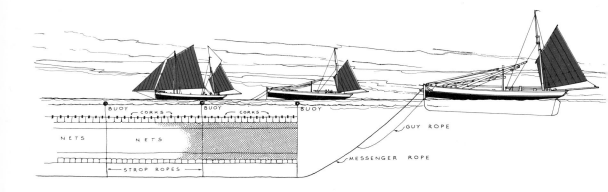

The drift net

an industrial discipline to fishing under sail and as far as the crews were concerned a
worsening of their lot. They were at sea for six or seven weeks at a time and ashore for
only one; the boxes, heavy with fish, had to be transferred at sea in heavy trawler's boats
to the steam carrier, a difficult and dangerous task in the open sea. Many smacks became
work-houses, without creature comforts, and the recruitment of crews became more
difficult, with a commensurate lowering of standards. But the introduction of the steam
trawlers had all but replaced sail by the First World War except at those ports such as
Brixham where a lack of facilities or other limitations did not attract the large investment
needed to establish a modern fleet.

The work of those who catch shoal-swimming fish is less spectacular than those of the
trawlers but it has a history much older, dating at least from medieval times. King of the
shoal fish is, or perhaps one must sadly amend was, the herring. All down the east coast of
the British Isles were fishing communities who relied upon it for a livelihood. The drift net
is, as the name implies, left free to drift with the tide, secured to the vessel at one end, a
buoy at the other end and supported along its length by floats. The distance it lay below
the surface varied according to the fishing area and the local traditions. A beach-boat
would carry a modest ten to twenty nets which joined together would form a 'fleet' and
could be three to five fathoms deep. The herring drifters worked at night because then the
nets were invisible to the surface-swimming fish. The mesh was adjusted so that small and
immature fish passed through the net and so stocks were conserved. Today the age-old
drift net has been replaced by huge trawls which sweep up every fish that swims and make
no distinction between mature and immature fish. The results are that while once Yarmouth quays were lined three and four deep with drifters, today they are almost empty.
Herring once concentrated in shoals around the coast in regular patterns beginning with a
gathering in the waters off Shetland in early summer. They worked their way along the
coast until at the end of November they had passed Lowestoft. Great fleets of drifters
congregated to capture the shoals and ashore the barrelling, salting, packing, smoking and
export required an industry which supported thousands. Long after the days of sail whole
Scottish East Coast families would travel to East Anglian ports and while father and the
sons fished the womenfolk worked at gutting and packing the catch. Northwards a similar
transhumance took place, to Wick and to Lerwick in the Orkneys.

The shores of southern England and off certain coasts of Ireland the mackerel swims in
shoals which, if they do not rival in size those of the herring, are substantial enough to be

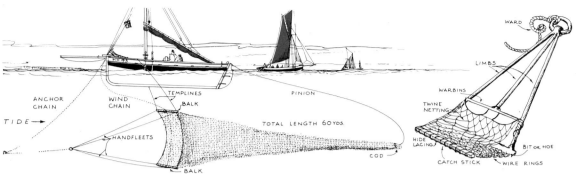

Stow net in use   Oyster dredge

captured with drift-nets. The nets used for mackerel have a slightly larger mesh but, just like the herring boats of the East Coast, they are used at night; and the luggers were designed to lower their masts easily and with a 'watch-mizzen' set, lie-to quietly awaiting the dawn.

The little sprat makes up in numbers for his diminutive size. These were caught in the Thames Estuary, where they appear in late autumn, by a stow-net. It was a form of fishing which had defeat built into the endeavours of those that practised it. More frequently than with other fish a good catch would bring a fall in price down to a derisorily low level, so that many farmers' fields in Kent and Essex have grown rich with the sprats spread on them as manure. The same fields might well be found to be drained by long, narrow lines of shells, remains of crustacea fished from the Thames and used to make Cockney Bank Holidays happier.

The long stocking-shaped net of the stow-boaters has a medieval feel about it. Suspended beneath an anchored smack it awaited the great densely-packed shoals and was then heaved aboard. The two great baulks, which maintained the net open at its mouth, proving a particularly intransigent piece of equipment to handle in the bleak weather that late autumn can bring, still leaving the fishermen to deal with the catch. This could threaten to sink the smack as it slithered into the hold if the seas had been particularly lavish and the sail back to harbour was a hard one. Small wonder that it is a method of fishing that has been left behind with fewer regrets than most.

Life afloat

The master of a small coasting schooner had a secure status in the community of which he was a member. He dressed when ashore in a manner appropriate to his undoubted respectability. When he went aboard he was rowed out and then descended into his cabin aft, only to re-emerge when all was ready for sea. At the other extreme was a boy, newly recruited to a Grimsby sailing trawler, bound for the Dogger Bank, who worked all the hours that were required of him. He had little more than the work-house clothes in which he came aboard and inhabited a floating wooden slum. Between these two extremes of existence there was a wide range of rewards and living conditions but, except for the few most fortunate, for all who earned their living at sea in sailing craft it was a life dominated by unremitting physical exertion. Setting sail, scraping paint, heaving on lines, standing lookout, coiling warps, working out the cargo and taking in reefs were part of a seemingly never-ending round of toil. Small wonder that the majority of those who experienced a life at sea in small sailing vessels looked upon the introduction of engines in trading craft and steam power in drifters and trawlers as nothing but a blessing. But if the old life held few compensations and less profit, even when viewed in retrospect by those who knew it at first hand, they were all proud of their skills and the ability they had developed to survive it.

These skills had to be learnt from an early age. While the time-honoured tradition of apprenticeship had been officially ended for seamen by the mid-nineteenth century it still continued for fishermen. A boy at thirteen would join the fishing smacks as the most junior member of the crew at a wage of a few shillings a week. His primary task was to coil down the trawl-warp in the black, dripping wet of the warp-room each time the trawl was hauled. Above him the clink, clink of the pawls on the barrel and the hiss of the steam winch reminded him that there was a world outside the dark hold as the work ground on for an hour, perhaps two. In between this he peeled potatoes, packed fish in boxes, washed down the deck after the catch had been sorted, rang the ship's bell during fog, and looked for the tea-kettle halliards. Life on a sailing barge for the third hand was less grim, but he was paid on the basis of a miniscule weekly wage. A boy on a smack had a proportionally small, but nevertheless real, share in the profits of the voyage and how many of them, giddy and sick in the stinking warp-room, as the smack rolled and pitched, were supported by dreams of how it would accumulate and then be spent on shore at the end of the voyage? A spritsail barge's third hand was officially cook and only took his spell at the wheel under the critical eye of the skipper. His day began at six with scrubbing the cabin floor, preparing breakfast and polishing the skipper's boots, but he usually spent the night undisturbed unless a crisis occurred on deck. Having proved his worth he could look

The open hold of the trow *Alma*, built at Gloucester in 1854 and rebuilt in 1916. The photo shows the side-cloths supported by iron stanchions and lined with boards to protect the open hold. She was the last trow to trade under sail. (H. O. Hill)

forward to an opportunity to become a mate, with a share in the profits from a freight, by the time he was eighteen and then perhaps a skipper at twenty.

A sailing vessel normally running in the home trade only required a master qualified by experience, so that a boy aboard a ketch or big coasting barge could eventually become skipper without passing an official written examination. Smacksmen were required to obtain an official certificate if they were to command a trawler of 25 tons or more. Older

The three-masted topsail schooner *Mary Miller*, built at Carrickfergus in 1881 and long owned at Fowey. She was one of the last three engineless schooners to trade in British coastal waters. (Graham Gullick)

men, who had earned by experience the right to command were issued with documents confirming their position which inevitably became known as 'certificates of servitude'. Smack insurers also issued certificates to masters of trawlers.

The huge number of spritsail barges provided a ready ladder of advancement and a lad who became weary of being a 'farmyard sailor', voyaging no further than the Estuary, could approach a skipper whose ketch-barge would take cargoes down the Rhine or to the Bristol Channel. Securing a berth as a seaman he would then join that company whose watchword was 'a wet shirt and a happy heart'.

The voyages down Channel, particularly in winter time were always testing to both ships and men. Days and nights were spent anchored sheltering in the Downs, with the

The *Emily* of Bridgwater, a small ketch, lost in the Bristol Channel in 1934, loaded with coal for her home port. She was built at Chepstow in 1895. (N.P.A.)

The schooner *Katie*, dried-out preparatory to tarring. Built at Padstow in 1881, she was the last two-masted topsail schooner trading along our coast and was at work until 1940. (Author)

Goodwins close at hand, waiting. There were nights when anchor-watch had to be kept on deck, with all hands ready when the tide turned and the likelihood of the anchor dragging became serious. Third hands were expected to take their spell at the windlass as the anchor was hove up when at last it was possible to get under way, and the cable was brought laboriously up and stowed in the chain locker. At least most smacks were fitted with a steam capstan by the eighties which provided not only a source of power but warmth as well. Before its introduction a wooden capstan was used to haul in the trawl, turned by bars against which the crew heaved, their feet trying to find a grip upon the wet deck. On the drifters a tribe of wretched casual workers was recruited, often at the last minute before sailing, to do this work. This recruitment of untrained men was a source of real danger, particularly on the East Coast of Scotland, for they could not be expected to master the skills of sailing and tended to impede those who had.

There was no galley as such aboard a smack and food was prepared on a coal stove in the cabin and eaten on a locker from deep tin plates which defied the swaying of the ship. One genius devised a kettle which, resembling a large tin boot, could be put into the little boiler furnace beneath the steam winch and rapidly provide hot water for tea. Aboard the ketches and schooners the galley was often a small hutch-like box, fixed on deck amidships, by iron straps and bolted to the deck. This enabled it to be removed for repairs or in the event of a deck-cargo being carried, but it was all too vulnerable to a heavy sea coming aboard. Each side of the galley was provided with a sliding door so that the cook could provide a very necessary ventilation by opening the leeward one. Many of these galleys

40

Built in 1875 the Cowes ketch *Arrow* traded between the Isle of Wight and the mainland until 1938, owned by Shepard Bros. of Newport. (Beken of Cowes)

Three schooners at Rosstrevor Harbour, Northern Ireland, *c.* 1880. The smaller is the *Margaret and Peggy* typical of the smaller Irish Sea schooners that were built with a sharp stern. (Robert Malster)

were so restricted that it was impossible for the occupant to stand upright and he sat on a wooden seat and juggled with his iron pots and pans wedged between the stove and his coal bunker. At least the frequency with which coal was carried as a cargo ensured that there was little shortage of fuel and it provided a ready, if unofficial, currency for barter with passing fishermen and craft less favoured, who might be lying alongside when in port.

Food on the sailing coasters was generally better than that provided, with strict adherance to Board of Trade regulations aboard deepsea square-riggers and certainly superior to a contemporary farm labourer's. On a coaster or smack the crew of four or five ate together, the skipper presiding. Ketches and schooners had a mess-room aft and the main meal was, if possible, timed so that one of the crew could be left on deck alone at the wheel. Roast leg of mutton, potatoes baked, boiled, peeled or unpeeled, cabbage (the first day out anyway) preceded by a suet duff or dumplings with gravy were usual. These were served first, for they took the edge off the men's appetite before the more expensive part of the meal was presented. Fried duff filled up the stomach before a morning spent at work on the cargo winch and eeked out the traditional bacon. Dried salt cod made up many of the cargoes that were carried by schooners from Newfoundland to Europe. This found its way on to the cabin table and was notoriously common on Welsh-owned schooners. Salt-beef was kept aboard trading craft in one or two large brass-bound casks, within easy reach of the galley and locked against the unauthorised. Sides of beef were bought and salted down in the casks and due to the constant movement of the vessel churning the contents it was considered a desirable commodity. It was not uncommon for pieces to be sold to shore-folk who sought it out along the quaysides where the schooners lay. The

42

only other form of preservation available for a fresh leg of beef or mutton was to tow it astern in a net!

Ship's biscuits, sometimes referred to as 'Portmadoc pantiles', a passing reference to the home port of a great fleet of sailing vessels and an indication of the article's texture, were reserved for the time when fresh bread was not available. It was said that one side of the biscuit was smooth and on this the crew spread their butter; the other side was deckled and recessed and was reserved for the exclusive use of skippers and mates! But the accepted method of messing was essentially egalitarian and did much to assist in maintaining the crew's spirit.

The masters of small coasters, from tiny West Country barges to ketch-barges loading 250 tons, were often part-owners. They were naturally inclined to keep a close watch upon the expenses their ship incurred, whether it was paint or potatoes. Food was an important expense, for the crew were usually paid by the voyage or month and food was found by the owners. But a mean skipper soon found himself with an inferior crew or none at all for word rapidly passed round the narrow world of the coasting fleet where ships often lay wind-bound for days in groups and the crews regularly met in waterside pubs. A factor which assisted in the perpetuation of the small sailing coaster when it had in actual fact ceased to be an economic proposition, lay in the form its ownership took. They were owned by groups of individuals, each having a proportion of the 64 shares into which, by long tradition, the investment in a ship was divided. These owners were invariably closely connected with the seafaring aspect of the little ports from whence the ships came. Butchers, chandlers and sailmakers looked to make a profit not merely from their position as share-holders in the enterprise but as suppliers of beef, rope and new mainsails to the ships in which they held shares. A master who cut down his meat bill could be met with questions from an offended share-holder as well as a grumbling crew.

Calms brought little respite from work aboard either coasters or smacks. It usually contrived to make the skipper irritable, for coasters were then at the mercy of the tide and could actually lose ground while smacks could not trawl. There was then painting to be done, iron work to be chipped, gear to be overhauled and on a fishing-boat nets to be repaired, new ones to be braided and fenders made from worn rope. If the weather was warm bedding was brought out to dry, for the forecastle, in the bows, where the crew slept was under the windlass. This took the weight of the vessel when it plunged and bucked at anchor in heavy weather, only partly relieved of its burden by rope springs and tackles. The deck around it became strained and inevitably leaked as the seas taken over the bow streamed across. It leaked on to the canvas frame folding bunks below and into the lockers, producing a wet misery, only partly relieved by the coal stove maintained at full blast. One task which frequently employed the crew, when the opportunity occurred in port, was the heating of a tar pot on the stove and running hot tar into the more obvious of the gaps in the seams of the deck planking directly above their quarters. The skipper and mate were more fortunate. Living aft they each had a small cabin which were to port and starboard of the main mess room; each was fitted with a bunk with drawers beneath and a glass deck-light above. Only the tread of the helmsman above and the grating of the rudder and the chains of the steering gear disturbed them below.

The accumulations of smacks on the fishing grounds which arose by the adoption of 'fleeting' towards the end of the sailing trawler's reign gave rise to the 'coper'. These were vessels fitted out in Continental ports and carrying cargoes of cheap duty-free liquor and tobacco which they peddled round the areas where the smacks fished, seeking customers amongst the concentrations of vessels awaiting the fish carriers. The results of their

Littlehampton's yard of Harvey built many wooden vessels concluding with ketch-barges like the *Clymping* of 121 tons launched in 1909. In 1930, in company with two others of a similar type, she sailed across the Atlantic to work on the Berbice River in British Guiana. (F. W. Spry)

salesmanship could be catastrophic. It was not unknown for crews to be so bemused with drink that they were incapable of facing tests of seamanship which were difficult enough to master when sober and which the Dogger always had in store. British ships also took part in the trade until trawler owners prevailed upon those who insured them to refuse cover. Men aboard the smacks, without ready cash, parted with sound gear and sails in exchange for drink, further endangering their own situation. The root of the problem lay not only in the availability of the cheap alcohol, but in the miserable existence of the men, away from home for six to eight weeks aboard a comfortless vessel. The foundation of the Mission to Deep Sea Fishermen did much to improve the immediate situation. Eventually in the teeth of opposition from the Customs, they found a way of obtaining permission to sell duty-free tobacco from their own specially equipped Mission smack and also provided much needed medical assistance. The shadow of death from drowning was one under which fishermen habitually worked and accepted stoically; but incapacity resulting from industrial accidents was much more common. The North Sea gave little opportunity for any help to be found for a man with badly crushed hands or fractured limbs. Illness was treated at first with suspicion and then with improvised medicinal cures which only worsened the situation; finally the application of neat alcohol was resorted to. Cruising amongst the smacks in all weathers, the Mission trawlers provided free medical and surgical treatment aboard by skilled hands. It must have been one of Victorian Britain's most worthwhile examples of practical Christianity. Eventually the 'copers' were driven from the sea as the result of the International Convention of 1893, but the fine work of the Mission continued. When the first collections and money from the sale of tobacco to smacksmen at sea was paid in to a Yarmouth bank the manager insisted that it was boiled before counting it.

The longshoremen were the peasants of the coast. They lived an independent existence in so far as they were self-employed but they were ground between the middle-men who purchased their catch and the sea that washed against their threshold. Like the fishermen who 'went deepsea' their existence was made tolerable by close family ties and an unwritten rule of help-one-another. The equipment they used, the nets, lines and boats, were of the simplest and the seaworthiness of the boats was restricted by the fact that they were launched from the beach. While the grandfathers of those who come within the scope of this book were undoubtedly subsidised by smuggling on a large and profitable scale, by the end of the nineteenth century this was all but extinguished. An efficient Coastguard Service, combined with the less obtrusive but equally effective village policeman, had seen to that.

The longshoreman almost always married the daughter of a fisherman. How else would he find a partner who had the skills to braid nets, bait long-lines, make lobster and crab pots, search for bait along the mud-flats and rocks and smoke fish for sale? The development of the seaside, with the coming of the railways undoubtedly did much to assist the longshoremen to survive. It provided a ready market for prime fish which, with luck, he could supply direct. Gentlemen might require a boat in which they could go mackerel

The Deal lugger *Anne* trawling in the Downs. She has a lute stern added to her transom stern to allow more room for the trawl beam when it came aboard. (National Maritime Museum)

45

spinning while the less prosperous were anxious for a 'trip on the briny', a requirement which could be met at a time before officialdom had woven a tight net of safety regulations relating to pleasure boats. Less well placed longshoremen, on coasts remote from developing holiday resorts, existed by maintaining a vegetable plot and were not above combining casual farm work with seafaring.

How they ever accumulated the fifty pounds or more of capital, at least a year's earnings, to purchase a boat, defies an explanation. Boat builders, as we have seen, made little enough profit and were resigned to accepting payment by instalments spread over two or three seasons. Occasionally the seas do provide a bounty and a lucky catch made when it evades others and the market is not flooded, brought a rare return in sovereigns. Sons travelled to the nearest port and saved a little from their wages as hands on the bigger drifters and smacks. Crewing aboard the yachts, which required a large complement of paid hands gave a chance to save. Just as daughters who went into domestic service returned to their homes with horizons widened and knowledge of other standards, so the sons who served on the racing craft were inclined to cast a critical eye over the ill-cut sails and blunt hull of the family lugger. If they stayed they did so on condition changes were made. Many were members of the Naval Reserve. It gives some insight into a longshoreman's life when one learns that the men considered the annual drills, at the remuneration of one pound a week conducted aboard the guard-ships around the coast, were a paid holiday.

Deal hovelling luggers drawn up ready to be launched down the sloping beach, *c.* 1865. The galley in the foreground contrasts with the much heavier second-class lugger *Sappho* and the even larger ones beyond. (Nat. Def. Photograph, Canada)

Preservation

The disappearance of sail has seen a growing keenness on the part of widely differing interests and individuals to preserve something of its beauty and lore before it is too late. It is a difficult task, far more complex than the preservation of old and valued buildings. The rapid development of ship-building technology has left few craftsmen who can undertake the necessary work to restore wooden ships and in the nature of things they will become fewer while the cost of traditional material, even if available, becomes prohibitively expensive. The craft that have survived and would make admirable subjects for restoration and preservation are all at least half a century old. Inevitably they have spent a long and arduous life. Patched and cheaply repaired, often caricatures of their former glory, they daunt the keenest enthusiast who would wish to preserve them.

But these enthusiasts exist and are growing in numbers. There are organisations set up in various ways to channel the wishes of individuals to contribute to preserving an old vessel, often with a localised interest, as an essential part of a region's character. The East Coast Sail Trust maintains both the *Thallata*, a mule-rigged sailing barge built in 1906 at Harwich, and the *Sir Alan Herbert*, built as the *Lady Daphne* in 1923. Both have auxiliary power, which was installed when they were still trading, but they have had their full rig carefully reinstated and their exterior appearance when underway at sea is little changed from the days when they were at work. The work they now do, acting as floating class-rooms in conjunction with schools, takes them all about the Thames Estuary. After a false start, a movement is stimulating the preservation of a Humber keel at Hull and another at York. The keel at Hull is the steel-built *Comrade* and so will avoid the difficulties inevitably involved in the maintenance of a wooden vessel. Better far a successful project involving a steel craft, which were numerous upon the Yorkshire waterways, than an effort which founders upon the insuperable problem of finding seasoned oak and shipwrights to use it. The *Albion*, maintained by the Norfolk Wherry Trust, sails the waterways of Broadland to show how cargoes were once carried on the Yare and the Bure.

The National Trust is involved with the restoration of the little West Country ketch *Shamrock*, built at Devonport in 1899. Together with the assistance of the National Maritime Museum, a formidable combination, it is hoped to preserve her at Cotehele Quay on the Tamar in Devon. It was at just such remote rural quays that the smallest of our sailing vessels delivered their cargoes. Also in Devon, the Exeter Maritime Museum of Boats concentrates upon preserving craft of many types, foreign as well as British, power as well as sailing, and maintains a large number ranging from a Welsh coracle to a coble and including a Bristol Channel pilot cutter.

It is the Maritime Trust that has shouldered the biggest burden with its object 'to restore, look after and put on display ships and equipment of interest and importance in the technical, commercial and military history of this country'. The work has gone ahead with exemplary energy and a number of vessels which relate to this book are now safely in the Trust's capable hands. The West Country topsail trading schooner *Kathleen and May*, built in 1900 at Connah's Quay in Flintshire, is open to the public in Sutton Harbour, the historic commercial port of Plymouth. The *Cambria*, a big wooden coasting spritsail barge, launched in 1906 and the last purely sailing vessel in north-west Europe to carry a commercial cargo, is under the protection of the Trust, with an exhibition illustrating the history and work of the spritsail barges of the Thames on display in the hold. The Trust also own the *Provident*, one of the last sailing trawlers built and although for many years a yacht, originally fishing from Brixham. She was launched in 1924 on the Dart and is at present on charter to the Island Cruising Club of Salcombe. The *Kindly Light*, a Bristol Channel pilot cutter built at Fleetwood in 1911 and later re-named *Theodora* when she did sterling work with the Ocean Youth Club, is to become the centrepiece of the Maritime Section of the National Museum of Wales at Cardiff. The Cornish fishing lugger *Barnabas* and the *Softwings*, a Falmouth oyster dredger, have also been saved for posterity. The *Barnabas* although later fitted with a motor was built in 1880 and will be restored to appear as she did when launched and sailed to the Scillies and Irish Sea to net mackerel.

An unsolved difficulty is that all these craft must lie at rest, sails unbent, most of the running rigging sent down, and the cabin stove cold. Except where size permits their use for exhibition purposes their holds are empty. Only very sympathetic care can at once preserve their individuality and authenticity and make them attractive to visitors and stimulating to the imagination of the young. For such superb vessels as the *Cutty Sark*, her three square-rigged masts towering above a graceful hull safe in its own dry-dock, this presents fewer problems; although it must be said that the tread of tens of thousands of visitors can produce wear that the seven seas could not. The appeal of small craft is subtler, bereft of their canvas filling with the wind and away from their natural element, much is irretrievably lost.

This problem of preserving working craft at work has been solved, at least to some extent, by another band of enthusiasts, individuals whose energy and persistence leaves one humbled. They are dedicated to restoring old fishing luggers, smacks and barges, learning from the remaining professionals the secrets of how best to sail them and use their traditional fishing gear effectively. The work of Michael Frost is exemplary in this field. He has with immense care and considerable expense rebuilt the one hundred and fifty year old *Boadicea* of Maldon so that she is ready to face another century afloat. Others have restored Bawley boats, Whitstable oyster yawls, Colne smacks and the Itchen ferry punt *Fanny* of Cowes, another centenarian. The little scaffie *Seaspray* sails from Stonehaven and a small fifie from Burghead, on the Scottish east coast. All these craft have the advantage of being of a manageable size for the amateur to be able to restore, maintain and then reap the richly deserved reward of enjoying sailing. Then, appropriately dressed he and she, can indicate a fully justified superiority over the yachtsman in his twentieth-century plastic aquatic caravan.

Museums

The Water Transport Section of the Science Museum, South Kensington, London, has an unequalled collection of local coastal and fishing craft. The National Maritime Museum, Greenwich, devotes Gallery 13 to the smaller British sailing vessels 1870–1920 and to estuary and river craft, while its Neptune Hall has much of interest in the same field.

The Scottish Fisheries Museum at Anstruther is growing and will maintain actual fishing craft. At Grimsby there is the Doughty Museum, which has an interesting collection of fishing vessels in model form while Hull's Museum of Fisheries and Transport at Pickering Park contains both models and paintings. Sunderland Museum has an excellent and well-documented collection of paintings of small trading vessels. The Norfolk Museum Service maintains an excellent maritime museum at Yarmouth, appropriately enough in the converted Seamen's Home. Nearby Lowestoft's small but valuable Maritime Museum, lovingly cared for, is an example for all old seaport towns to follow. Exeter Maritime Museum preserves a wide range of British and foreign craft, many afloat and fully rigged, and there is much of interest at the old Custom House Museum at Poole, recently established.

North Deal boatmen wearing the traditional seal-skin caps, and knitted guernsey and canvas smock of the nineteenth-century longshoreman. Photos by Paul Martin 1886. (V. and A. Museum)

The Spritsail Barge

The spritsail barge of the Thames survived to be the very last of all the seagoing commercial sailing vessels of North West Europe. Its tall spars, the purposeful solidarity of its hull and its grace under sail combined to provide for a generation to whom the sailing ship was unknown, a living experience of the past. Perhaps the most important factor contributing to her outlasting her contemporaries was that a 'sprittie', loaded with a 170 tons cargo, could be sailed by a crew of two. Moreover the hull of a barge was relatively cheap to construct, with its box-section and the restricted use of expensive, naturally grown, wooden crooks. It had evolved from the Thames river lighters and the retention of the lighter's huge hatches enabled the sailing barge to accommodate modern cargo machinery. The handling of a barge by such a small crew is made possible by its spritsail rig. We may use the present tense in talking of the spritsail barge for fortunately a number of them, almost unaltered from how they appeared when in trade, are still preserved. The

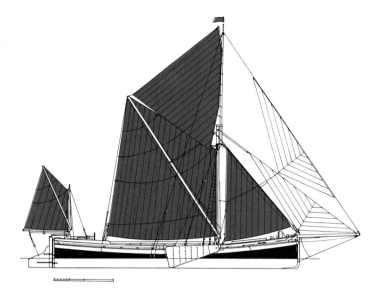

large mainsail remains aloft and is furled by brails which are ropes that draw up the sail to the mast like a theatre curtain. A sprit makes it possible for the topsail to remain set, although the main is furled, enabling a barge to be manoeuvred under a minimum of canvas. Both foresail and mainsail are sheeted to a horse, fitted across the full width of the hull, so that when going about they do not require tending by the crew. The heel of the bowsprit, like the foot of the mast, is secured in a tabernacle and may be steeved up vertically to avoid causing trouble in the congested docks. The diminutive mizzen mast is similarly set up in an iron tabernacle and may be lowered for negotiating bridges. When going about in narrow waters the mizzen assists in swinging round the long hull of the barge.

Spritsail barges were built of widely differing tonnages, but to an almost identical pattern. The smallest, some 40 ft. overall worked about the East Anglian rivers, serving farm quays and loading 30 tons. At the opposite extreme were two hundred tonners trading coastwise, with a range between Exeter and Hull; they were almost 90 ft. overall. All carried lee-boards; the barge's flat bottom had no exterior keel and a large barge drew only seven or eight feet when loaded; unloaded they drew between three and four feet and one of their major advantages was that they could sail without ballast. Raised and lowered by small iron winches on the quarters, the lee boards were essential if a barge was to work well to windward.

As the Metropolis grew during the nineteenth century the barges brought stone, bricks and timber to the Thames. They then supplied London's daily requirements; hay and straw for its thousands of horses, flour and malting barley, cement and sand. They distributed cargoes from dockland to the small ports which big steamers disdained and worked in trades which were centuries old, such as carrying stone from the quarries at Portland and bringing material for the maintenance of the sea-walls all about the wide estuary. Unlike other coastal and estuary craft the barges numbers were not counted in scores but thousands. Many were owned in fleets, each with a distinctive 'bob', the bargeman's house flag. But each barge retained an individuality, even those, and there were many, which were built of steel from an identical draught. The decoration of the broad transom stern and the bow badge, a wooden block on either side of the stem-head, always showed a lively originality.

The Stumpie Barge

While her bigger and more resplendently rigged sisters were built and owned along the length of the East and South-Eastern coast, the little stumpie barge was essentially a Cockney craft. Its home was the grimy waters of the Thames tideway and the oily creeks and canals that led off it into London's less salubrious industrial areas. Although occasionally a tempting freight might take a stumpie further afield (it is said one reached King's Lynn) the usual limits of her trade were represented by a line drawn between Shoeburyness, just below Southend and the North Foreland.

Their name derived from the fact that they never carried a topmast. Almost every voyage took them 'above bridges' and this required lowering the mast to deck level which was made much easier without the topmast and its attendant gear. As the stumpies worked almost entirely within the limits of the industrial Thames and Medway and all movement was at the behest of the tide, the loss of performance due to the absence of a topsail was not serious. Indeed, until 1889 stumpie barges competed in the annual barge matches sailed on the Thames and Medway and gave a good account of themselves, although the best amongst them augmented their sail-plan by setting a bowsprit and jib.

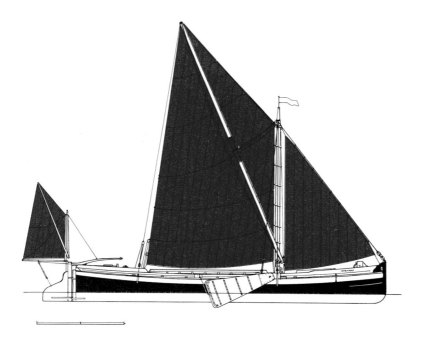

For work 'above bridges' a short mast was set up with a lug-sail. This together with backbreaking work on the sweep, the name for a long oar worked from the bow, gave sufficient steerage-way over the tide. The bridge lug-sail could be pressed into service and set when running before the wind in the manner of a spinnaker.

They perpetuated the rig of the earliest barges on the Thames and like them many retained a tiller for steering, with the mizzen sail mounted on the rudder head.

The smallest of the stumpies were known as the Cut Barges and traded to the Regent and Surrey canals with building materials. They had an average capacity of 70–80 tons and as little as a 14 ft. beam. Working up to Paddington, on the Regents Canal, a tunnel had to be negotiated and the bargemen lay on their backs and legged the barge through. These barges were built with hardly any sheer and even the windlass bitts were cut off as short as possible. Lee-boards were unshipped for these inland journeys and the wooden handles were removed from the cast-iron steering wheel to gain a few inches. Sometimes the hold was partly flooded on the return journey, for without a cargo the barge could not pass under a particularly low bridge, and then the water ballast had to be pumped out. Life on a stumpie did not provide much opportunity for heroism but ingenuity and hard work were always required. Another even smaller class of stumpie worked on the river Lee, employed carrying explosives.

Stumpies normally handled the least glamorous cargoes. London provided endless refuse for transportation to the marshes down river; bricks and cement were delivered from Kent and Essex, while timber loaded from steamers in the docks was distributed about the estuary. Despite their humble calling their appearance was far from dowdy. The stumpies always had a sprit which was proportionately longer than those of the topsail barges, and it was painted with contrasting bands of colour about its centre. Rails were blue, green or grey, blocks and quarter-boards white, and the transom was decorated in traditional style; a style borrowed from that of the more ornate Victorian public house. The mainsail was often emblazoned with the name and insignia of the owner.

The Boomie Barge

The boomie, or ketch barges were a successful attempt in the last days of coastwise sail to combine the economically constructed hull developed by the builders of spritsail barges and the rig of a sea-going vessel. Many were launched for the North East coast coal trade to replace the schooners and brigs. The boom-sail barges were rigged as ketches, as the name implies, their mainsail was of the normal gaff and boom type, while the mizzen was stepped well inboard to give ample room for the movement of the fifteen foot tiller. The first of these barges was launched from the eighteen fifties onwards and building went on until 1919, when the last was constructed at Rye. The earliest had square topsails and topgallants and the full headgear associated with a bowsprit and jib-boom. These craft carried fully 200 tons of coal, which were loaded at the Tyneside staithes and then discharged by basket and winch at one of a score of little ports or rural quays which were unaffected by steamships capturing the coal-trade elsewhere.

While the earlier and larger boomies had an attractive counter stern and a gammon-knee at the bow, blending the lines of the hull with the bowsprit, many had no such pretensions to maritime grace and were, in fact, the most economical form of coasting sailing vessel developed. Their ketch rig was made more efficient by the fitting of roller

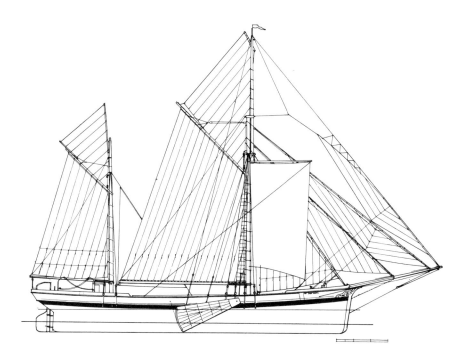

reefing gear. This replaced the traditional system of point-reefing and while it tended to strain and eventually distort the sail its use saved much effort on the part of the crew. By reducing the crew to a minimum it was possible to send a boom-sail barge loading 250 tons to sea with a crew of four or even three.

Life on a boomie barge was by no means easy, for heaving out the cargo was usually considered to be part of the job. The forecastle was roomy, there was rarely any shortage of coal to heat it and the skipper's accommodation aft, where all the crew ate, was often lined with mahogany and had its gentility emphasised by a neat black-leaded fire-grate. The larger boomies carried a small wooden galley on deck, where food was cooked and the wheelhouse provided a lavatory. A substantial boat was carried in davits on the quarter and many of the boomies were fitted with a patent pump-handle windlass, a more appropriately sea-going piece of equipment than those on a sprittie, which were turned by handles. They had hatches which were proportionately much larger than those of the round-bottomed schooners they replaced, and which simplified loading and unloading. Boomies were undoubtedly good sea-boats and could stand any weather the North Sea and Channel could offer when properly handled. Unlike even a big spritsail barge, where the weight of the sprit and its sails remains aloft, well reefed down, a boomie would lie-to comfortably. For successful sailing, particularly when without a cargo, although like the spritsail barge they needed no ballast, the boomies were crippled without lee-boards and these were always fitted. They were essential for working, tack and turn about, in narrow waters.

Besides the coal, the boomies carried a wide variety of cargoes. Tree trunks, road stone from the Channel Isles, tiles and bricks, deck-cargoes of timber and Cornish clay all figure in old cargo-books. A regular trade was to Remagen, far up the Rhine, for bottled mineral water and then, having delivered them to the Thames, returning with the empties. The very last boomie, the *Martinet,* built at Rye in 1912, sank off the Suffolk coast in 1941.

The Mulie Barge

The mulie-rigged barge, as its name indicates, was a barge rigged in such a way as to combine elements of both the ordinary spritsail barge and those of the ketch barge in order to produce a profitable vessel. The mulie had a hull with a fine sheer and substantial rails, raised fore and aft by bow and quarter boards. It had a sprit mainsail which enabled it to be handled by a crew of two men and a boy; but the size of the mainsail was proportionately smaller than that of the normal spritsail barge for the mizzen was well forward of the wheel and set on a gaff and boom. Like the mainsail the mizzen was brailed in against the mast.

Although a few of the ketch-barges were launched with masts that lowered so that they could work 'above bridges', most had their masts stepped in the keelson, in the manner of a seagoing ship. The masts of the mulie barges were set in tabernacles on deck and could be lowered. While their rigging was heavy, four shrouds on either side of the mast and double topmast stays were usual, it was as adaptable as that on a much smaller spritsail barge. The jib of a mulie was always hanked to a stay and stowed with gaskets on the end of the bowsprit; many had a number of lines rigged between the bowsprit shrouds to provide some help to the mate dowsing the jib when it was lowered and to prevent the sail from being swept under the spar. The bigger mizzen mast enabled the mulies to set a mizzen staysail, hoisted from the mizzen masthead and the tack of the sail was secured to a ring-bolt on the hatch-combing. Some contrived a mizzen yard-topsail and even a

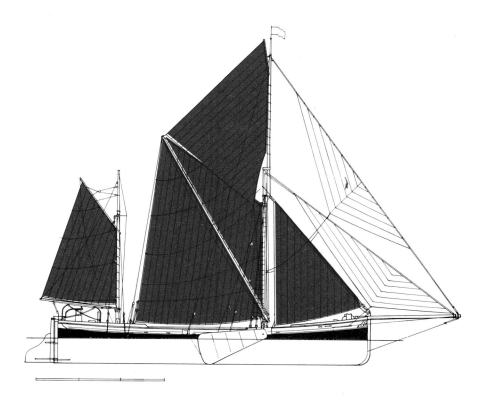

squaresail. When a skipper had before him the prospect of a long haul with, for instance, 180 tons of coal and was bound from the Humber to Poole, he did his best to make the most of a fair wind.

The Newcastle coal trade faded away, as far as sail was concerned, but coal continued to be shipped from the Humber to the smaller ports until the nineteen fifties, by spritsail barges. The mule-rigged barges could cope well enough with these voyages and as they required a smaller crew than the ketches, they gradually replaced them. A number of the smaller boomies were converted to spritsail rig, some retaining their fixed bowsprit and headsails. The majority were fitted with a substantial wheel-house aft which gave a welcome protection to the helmsman. An iron winch to port of the mast-case handled the main-brails for furling the mainsail and took the topsail halliards. To starboard a winch was provided for the foresail halliard and another barrel took the wire rope for raising the bowsprit. Coasting barges always had ratlines on both port and starboard shrouds.

No account of the mule-rigged spritsail barges is complete without a mention of the score or so of fine steel vessels built after the First World War. Most renowned of these was the quartet launched at Yarmouth 1925–26 and owned on the Thames. They were nearly 100 ft. overall, loaded about 300 tons and were crewed by two men and a boy. Although they set 5,600 square feet of working canvas they were relatively snugly-rigged for coastwise work in winter. One, the *Will Everard,* now re-named, survives as a yacht and another the *Ethel Everard* was left on the Dunkirk beaches.

One of the few remaining mulies, the *Thalatta,* is still at work with her full rig and is smartly maintained; she is owned by the East Coast Sail Trust and acts as a seagoing classroom for young people.

The Thames Bawley

The type of fishing craft most closely associated with the Thames estuary was the bawley-boat. Its tall sail plan was distinguished by a standing gaff, long bowsprit and a boomless mainsail which enabled the crew to work on deck with the minimum danger of being swept overboard. The standing gaff was an arrangement which had a long tradition of use on smaller trading and fishing craft in the Thames estuary although a bawley's gaff was lowered to a few feet above deck-level when work was done. The bawley's unusual name is almost certainly a corruption of 'boiler-boat'. They were miniature factory ships, processing their own catch of brown shrimps as soon as it was emptied from the trawl, in a cast-iron copper which was lashed down in a well amidships. Left until they reached the mooring the catch would soon lose its savour. The approach of a fleet of bawleys making for port was heralded by a fresh aroma of briskly burning coal fires and the salty tang of cooking crustacea.

The bawleys developed from an earlier half-decked clinker-built craft of some 22 ft., but carrying a similar rig to the latter-day examples. During the second half of the nineteenth century they grew in size and numbers as the trippers to Southend and Margate proliferated, seeking sea-food to stimulate their thirst, until the last of the bawleys were boldly shaped vessels of over ten tons and nearly 40 ft in length. Harwich, was the

extremity of the bawley's domain on the northern shore of the Thames estuary while Leigh on Sea, close by Southend, was their traditional stronghold. From Leigh they went cockling on the wide mud banks of the Thames. There were also fleets at Gravesend, at Rochester, and occasionally Margate in the summer formed their base.

Most bawleys lay on the mud at their moorings and for this reason they were strongly built to withstand pounding when they grounded and constructed with a considerable beam so that they could provide a good working space on deck. They all had a wide, shallow transom and the stern-post was nicely raked in the large Brightlingsea and Harwich craft, which also tended to have a deeper draught. The Leigh bawleys which had to negotiate a narrow, winding creek to land their catch, were shallower and their stern, like the stem, was vertical. Besides shrimping in the summer the bawleys went trawling for bigger game and in the autumn stow-boating for sprats, a hard living earned anchored in the dark, unsheltered waters of the estuary. The loose-footed mainsail was reduced in area by brailing – a rapid method of regulating sail area to a nicety when trawling. Above the mainsail a jib-headed topsail was carried on a lofty topmast and was stowed aloft. The foresail sheet ran on an iron horse and a variety of headsails were set ranging from a tiny spitfire jib to a huge balloon foresail for summer calms to keep steerage-way. On the fore-deck was a traditional heavy barrel-windlass, massive enough to heave in the out-sized anchor employed when stow-boating. The trawl was brought home by the 'wink', a winch set on a stout post, secured against the fore-coaming of the hatch.

Bawleys were used by syndicates of pilots and over the years many were purchased for conversion to yachts. Few yachtsmen, however, could resist fitting a boom to the mainsail and inevitably with this some of the bawley's essential character was lost. More recently examples such as the *Bona* and *Auto de Fe* have been rebuilt and re-rigged in the authentic tradition after years of servitude as motor craft.

The Medway Doble

The Medway doble was the Kentish river's counterpart of the Thames Peter-boat which was once used for fishing above bridges on London's river and long since extinct. Unlike the Peter-boat the doble has survived, but only in a motorised form. In construction the dobles are exactly similar bow and stern and the beam was never less than one-third of its length, usually 12 to 15 ft. Its double-ended design, while adapting it for rowing both backwards and forwards easily, suggests an ancestry that dates back to the fourteenth century, before any northern craft had their sterns differentiated from their bows. She is clench-built, with seven or eight moderately wide planks on either side and with substantial frames at wide intervals. There is a little deck fore and aft, just below the gunwale and a wide waterway runs along the side; the gunwale is well supplied with scuppers, so that the boat is kept reasonably dry when the nets are being hauled in and it has provision for a pair of oars. There is a miniature wet-well built in amidships for the storing of the catch. The water enters the wet-well from a centre-board case, for a number of the dobles were fitted with these contrivances to assist in working to windward. Either side of the well are spaces for stowing the nets.

The normal rig for a doble in the days before engines were fitted to them was a spritsail and a foresail, set flying, without a forestay and, in the tradition of most Thames sailing craft, working across an iron horse on the forward side of the fore-coaming. For simplicity's sake some discarded the typical spritsail rig in favour of a standing lug, particularly once a motor was installed. When moored everything could be easily unshipped and stowed fore and aft. The dobles and the smaller Peter-boats were never large enough for a cabin of even the most modest scale. Traditionally their owners spread a tilt

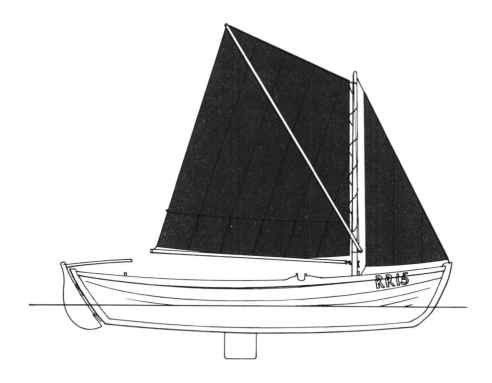

of tarred blanket over a framework of bent wood to provide some shelter when winter fishing. A few even arranged a tiny coal stove within, which gypsy-like, protruded a black chimney through the grimy covering.

Sometimes 'kofs', or floating fish boxes of perforated wood, were towed astern of the doble to contain the catch when it was too large for the wet-well aboard. The Peter-net that was used by the doble's crew was a seine net. Some 20 to 25 fathoms long, it was cast and then retrieved by the boat rowing a complete circle before gathering it in. The dobles also served to assist in setting stop nets across creeks and outfalls. These captured fish as they worked their way down on the ebbing tide, urged seaward by the fisherman thrashing the water with his oar.

Whitebait, an aristocratic dish provided by these humble little boats, once swam up as far as London Bridge, but pollution has long since driven them to the lowest reaches of the Thames. Whitebait were caught by seining or by a miniature stow-net, suspended a few feet below the surface of the water. Eels were captured by close-meshed nets, weighted at the bottom so that they rested on the bed of a creek, while the top was buoyed. Eels would strike the net, work their way along it, and then find themselves trapped in one of its pockets; the whole net being regularly emptied and re-set by the fishermen. Unlike whitebait, the eels are still with us, less susceptible to the insalubrity of our rivers.

The Essex Smack

The Essex smacks survived as sailing vessels, or low-powered auxiliaries, as late as 1939. The smacks were cutter-rigged fishing vessels, employed in a wide range of tasks; differing types evolved, but all had a basically similar hull-form and gear. Their relatively sophisticated appearance was brought about by the fact that many of their builders also constructed yachts, while the smacksmen themselves found employment in summer aboard the opulent pleasure craft of Victorian days. Brightlingsea, at the mouth of the Colne, was their stronghold while fleets were also owned further up the river at Rowhedge. At Burnham, at nearby Tollesbury and from half a dozen little waterside Essex villages there were groups of these attractive little craft with their tanned sails working about the creeks and estuaries. However, the Essex smack, although in its later years associated with narrow swatchways and shoal waters, had originally been developed to range far and wide. At the lower end of the hierarchy of the smacks were the little 10-ton boats which rarely left the limits of the estuary and whose principal occupation was dredging for oysters. This was done by dragging dredges across the beds to gather the shell-fish, a technique requiring special skills and a handy vessel, above all one which could then turn smartly to windward. Some of these little smacks were clench built and transom sterned, survivors of days before ideas of advanced design had affected the smack-builders; little more than 30 ft. long they were very beamy and did not usually

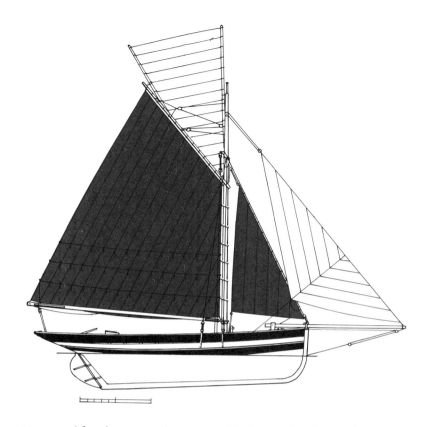

carry a topmast. After them came the more yacht-like smacks of around 15 tons and some 45 ft. overall, built with hollow bow waterlines, a long fine run to a nicely finished counter stern. Because they were essentially work-boats the free-board aft was low. The ballast was all carried in the hull and amidships was the fish hold; the crew lived in a diminutive cabin aft and the forecastle was reserved for spare sails and gear. Smacksmen always retained the simple handspike barrel windlass in the bows for anchor work, but fitted an iron-geared hand capstan to heave up the trawl. They trawled in spring as well as dredging for oysters and in winter set stow-nets for the huge shoals of sprats. Many were laid up in summer when their crews mustered for service as paid hands aboard the yachts.

Brightlingsea had the largest smacks of all, some were up to 40 tons and 65 ft. overall. They worked on the oyster beds off Jersey and the Dutch coast and much to the annoyance of the local fishermen they dredged oysters in Welsh bays and Norfolk creeks, in Scottish waters and Suffolk rivers. When the occasion arose they were used to import cargoes of French potatoes and Norwegian lobsters and acted as fish carriers to the trawler fleets in the North Sea. Salvaging, the Essexman's term for recovering goods and gear from wrecked ships, occupied both types of the larger smacks. It brought valuable hauls and the keels of many new boats were laid upon the proceeds of a profitable venture in this field. Events of the keenest competition, but conducted under pleasanter conditions, were the annual smack races. The first recorded race, which took place on the Blackwater, must surely be the earliest held for work-boats anywhere on our coast and dates from 1783. They were later held in the autumn, when the yachts were laid up and the smacks were fitted out and have been revived in recent years by amateur smacksmen with all the old enthusiasm.

The Southwold Beach Boat

The longshoreman's boat varied in detail but on the East and South coasts it had a basic similarity. It was clench-built, quite open, although some contrived a tiny cuddy in the bows, and between 15 and 22 ft. overall. They were driven by a powerful dipping lug and a mizzen set up on a long out-rigger. The tack of the mainsail was usually hooked to an iron bumkin, projecting from the stem to give the opportunity to set a larger sail. There were no shrouds to support the mast, but the halliard was always set up to weather, the only other rope was the down-haul for the sail. All the spars could be easily stowed within the length of the boat when, fishing done, it was drawn up on the beach.

The longshoremen were beach fishermen, working off the open shore, launching their little boats across greased skids of oak and then returning through the surf and hauling them up with the aid of an ancient capstan. Shingle ballast was carried, stowed in the bilges in small sacks and having the advantage of being easily disposed of over the side if the haul of fish was a good one. Longshoremen were men who were the masters of a great range of skills, learnt from childhood. They were, in turn, seamen, fishermen, bait-gatherers, net braiders, sail-makers, and shipwrights. They were their own salesmen; they cured fish, patched their houses, gleaned the tide-line and were on call for life-saving duty at sea. Their communities were tightly knit, for the longshoreman's wife must by necessity be skilled at baiting long lines, repairing nets, and have skills literally at her finger tips which a farm or town bred girl could not have had the opportunity to acquire.

The beach-boats were employed on a year-long calendar of fishing. While the lug-rig is not really well adapted for trawling, they contrived to trawl for shrimps; they also trawled

for roker and plaice, set long-lines, and laid down lobster-pots. With the summer visitors gone, the herring nets were taken out and then shipped to gather the herring harvest. Longshore herrings are particularly prized for although often caught within hailing distance of the beach, they are admirable fish for curing. Sprats, which could also be smoked, were a winter-time catch and came with such a prodigality that once the first flush was over they fetched prices which hardly covered the expense of the penny candles in the fisherman's lantern.

If the farm labourer, prior to the First World War, lived a life near the subsistence level, his brother the longshoreman was almost as badly off. It was only the fact that builders were prepared to spread the payment for a new boat over a long period that he could afford the tools of his trade. But several factors contributed to mitigate his lot. The development of 'the seaside' provided a lively summer market for prime fish, while the holidaymakers enjoyed the opportunity of a modest 'trip on the briny'. It was accepted that the young men went 'big-boating' from the nearest fishing harbour, where middle-water fishing vessels recruited crews from amongst longshoremen. Membership of the Naval Reserve, with its annual stipend and training period, helped to provide the lump sum for the replacement of gear.

Fitting motors into longshore boats began during the First World War and continued apace until today none is without one. The old boats, built originally for sailing, are now worn out. They have been replaced by wooden clench-built ones, constructed upon the same principle, but to a subtly different shape that is devised to be driven by a propeller.

The Lowestoft Sailing Drifter

During the closing years of the nineteenth century the East Coast sailing drifter reached its zenith. It earned the grudging admiration of fishermen everywhere and both the Dutch and French imitated its hull and rig. The smacks had evolved from heavy lug-rigged craft, clench-built, with a clumsy lute stern. The stimulus for their development came from the railway, establishing a link with a much wider market and greatly improved harbour facilities. Smack owners required a vessel that could use a drift-net and also, with the least possible trouble, be fitted out for trawling.

The lug-rig is not suitable for trawling; it is difficult to heave-to and when going about the constant dipping of the sail round the mast requires a skilful crew. The change began when some of the luggers fitted a gaff-mainsail, but retained the old rig mizzen. The mainsail did not have a boom, to facilitate work on deck when fishing. Above the mainsail a gaff topsail was set, called a 'jacky' at Lowestoft; this compensated for the rather stumpy proportions of the mast. Soon the gaff rig was in use on the mizzen. Both the main and mizzen were fitted with four rows of reef-points, the lower row was on a 'bonnet'; this was a detachable section of the sail, latched on by a series of loops. When the bonnet was removed from the mizzen sail it was then of a convenient size to keep the smack head to wind when lying to the nets.

Once the nets were shot the main mast was lowered and the masthead was lashed to the mizzen. Lowestoft-built drifters had bigger mizzens, which raked forward at an unusually

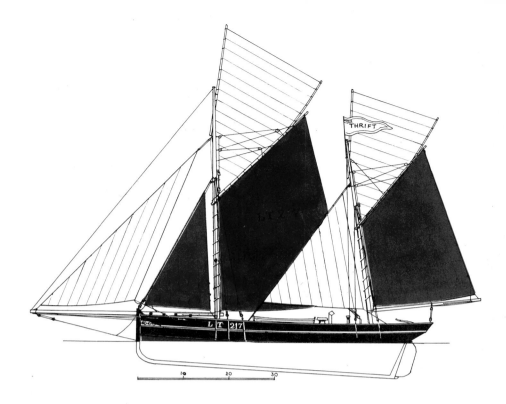

pronounced angle, while those on the Yarmouth boats were shorter, more upright and were without the decorative finial the Suffolk men liked. At the same time that the change in rig was taking place a change from clench to carvel construction began. At first only the topsides were planked in the carvel manner, for this allowed vessels to be closely packed in harbour with less danger of damage to one another. Then finally all the hull was carvel planked and terminated in an attractive round counter stern, although it was said clench-built bow enabled the smack to remain freer of water on deck.

Driftnet fishing began in spring for herring, but spring herring were poor, tasteless things and most of the catch went to provide bait for the boats that fished with long-lines. Then came the summer herring and mackerel fishery; alternatively some drifters sailed away to the Cornish ports, taking a pilot for the voyage and these fished from Penzance and Plymouth. Summer also saw East Anglian boats working from Shields, Scarborough and Grimsby for it was not profitable to sail back to Yarmouth to land a catch. They all gathered again at their home-port for the great herring fishery from September to November and then converted for trawling. A crew of six was carried when trawling and nine when fishing for shoal fish. They were away for two or three nights, but good hauls would bring a drifter back the day after it set out. The last of the sailing drifters were of up to 40 tons and some 60 ft. overall. The appearance of low-powered steam drifters in the eighteen nineties doomed the sailormen. The last two sailing drifters to be built at Lowestoft, the *Content* and the *Pretoria,* were launched in 1900. By the time the fishery revived after the First World War not one remained in commission.

The Yarmouth Shrimp Boat

The harbours at Yarmouth and Lowestoft developed as popular seaside resorts and gave employment to a numerous fleet of little shrimp boats. Their crews lived along the banks of the Yare and in the narrow Yarmouth 'rows' and moored their craft within a stone's throw of their homes. The seasonal nature of their work saw them employed in autumn as deck-hands on drifters, lumpers and wherrymen; in January they began to fit out their craft, scraping spars, tarring hulls, and repairing nets. The hulls of the Yarmouth shrimpers were about 21 ft. overall, beamy and clench-built of oak; built to last, for a well-constructed boat could serve three generations of fishermen. The transom stern was painted white and the iron-shod keel extended 12 ins. below the hull and was rockered, being noticeably deeper amidships.

A cuddy was built forward, equipped with a little coal stove and entered by a hatch on the foredeck. The foredeck was protected by a substantial wash strake, picked out in blue which gave the little shrimpers their characteristic profile. Aft of the cabin bulkhead was the mast tabernacle and two substantial thwarts. The helmsman worked a short tiller which passed under an iron horse, bolted to the transom. The shrimpers were often rowed and thwole pins were fitted in the gunwale.

The shrimpers were rigged with a simple sloop-rig. It retained its simplicity because they never shipped a crew of more than two and sometimes worked single-handed. The

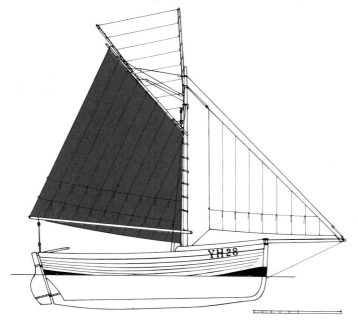

mast was supported by a single shroud on either side and a fore-stay, set up with a tackle at the extremity of the bowsprit. The boom of the mainsail did not have jaws or an iron swivel to attach it to the mast but was retained in position by a rope which encircled the mast and was belayed to a cleat on the upper side of the boom. The eye in the mainsail clew was held in an iron hook on the outboard end of the boom. These unorthodox methods all assisted in stowing the mast and gear, for many of the shrimpers had to regularly negotiate Yarmouth's bridges to reach their moorings. The mast was raised and lowered by the forestay. A yard topsail was set, extending well above the masthead and two staysails were carried aboard, the smaller for setting in a hard breeze.

Shrimping was carried out on the morning tide so that there might be fresh cooked shrimps available for the trippers' teas. The boats used two sorts of gear, the shrimp trawl and the beam net. The former had a beam of about 15 ft. with a fine mesh; in summer it was fitted with pockets, or 'peds', to capture any soles which might be disturbed as the trawl was drawn over the sea bed. The beam net was a type of dredge net, about 13 ft. long and without trawl-heads. The fishing grounds were around the Cockle light vessel and off Corton, but never further away from port than to make return to port on the half flood impossible. The trawl towrope or warp was always fastened forward of the shrouds and then tied in on the quarter in such a way that it would allow the craft to swing head to tie easily if the net should become fast upon some underwater obstacle. The grounds they fished were thick with obstacles, wrecks and old anchors predominating. Sorting the catch was done underway, sieving out the weed and rubbish only; the shrimps were not boiled aboard, except in a very few craft.

The appearance of the fleet's topsails in the Yare was a signal for the wives to light up the fires beneath the iron cauldrons in which the shrimps were prepared. Boiled in a brine solution, a quarter of a peck of salt to 2½ pails of water, the whole process had to be carefully supervised – too little or too long and the work of hours at sea was spoilt by the catch becoming too limp and soft. Correctly adjusted, the boiling and brine combined to be the Yarmouth brewers' best friend. The sailing shrimpers are now all worked with engines but still have a jaunty air and give a touch of colour to the banks of the Yare from which fishing has almost gone.

The Norfolk Wherry

The Broadland waterways were the home of the black-sailed Norfolk wherry. In its last years, for there were wherries sailing in the 'thirties, it shared the rivers with the butterfly pleasure craft which proliferated upon what, by then, had become a popular holiday area. To the wherrymen the waterways were a highway which linked Norwich with the ports of Yarmouth and Lowestoft and connected a hundred remote staithes and village quays. They loaded coal and deals, bricks and cement, oak for barrels, and reeds for thatching; they took barley to the maltings and beer to the riverside pubs.

The wherries were graceful, shallow craft, with a single hatch running the length of the hull, terminating at the stern with a little cabin equipped for her two-man crew. The mast at the forward end of the hatch pivoted between massive oaken cheeks and was counter-balanced with a lead weight. This enabled it to be lowered easily and then raised again with the minimum of effort when negotiating bridges. The mast was unsupported by shrouds and carried a gaff mainsail, without a boom and hoisted aloft by means of an ingenious combination of peak and throat halliards; the tail of the rope led to a winch at the foot of the mast.

Only rarely did wherries go to sea. Choosing their time they slipped out from Yarmouth and made a short salt-water voyage to Lowestoft. Sometimes they lightered cargoes out of ships anchored in Yarmouth Roads, this was an employment for the larger craft for

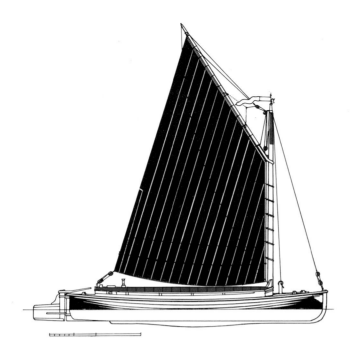

wherries varied considerably in size. Some were only 35 ft. overall, loading some 15 tons of cargo; the largest ever launched was the *Wonder*. No less than 84 tons of coal could be shot into her capacious hold. More typical would be a wherry of 58 ft. with a 15 ft. beam and drawing about five feet of water. Most of the later craft were sharp-sterned, with a small well for steering abaft the cabin, although a narrow transom stern had been common on smaller wherries. A number of steel wherries was built, but these were exceptional. The traditional construction was clencher; the shell of the hull, usually of fourteen two-inch oak planks each side, was formed around two or three temporary moulds and then the frames built in.

Wherries were equipped with an external keel, which did much to earn them the reputation of being able to sail closer to the wind than any other commercial craft, but this keel was made removable so that the draught might be reduced to a minimum. The keel was unbolted, heaved up to the surface, and then moored to the river's bank while the wherry negotiated the last few miles to her destination. On her return voyage the keel was manoeuvred under the hull and bolted securely in position. Wherry sails were always black, except for a short period of preliminary use, when the untreated canvas was allowed to stretch. It was then painted with a mixture of coal tar, herring oil, and lamp black; alternative sides of the sail were dressed at yearly intervals.

A distinctive feature of the wherry was its mast-head vane. These were individual to each wherry, but were essentially a frame supporting a full fathom of red bunting, balanced on the spindle by a painted metal silhouette of delightful invention. Dancing-girls, Lord Nelson, suns and stars, wheatsheafs, and mermaids all appeared.

In 1949 the Norfolk Wherry Trust was formed to preserve one of Broadland's typical traders. They obtained the wherry *Albion,* built in 1898, and she is to be seen sailing the rivers and Broads, an arresting reminder of the days that are gone.

The Yarmouth Beach Yawl

The beach yawl of Norfolk and Suffolk was a shore-boat built to an heroic mould. Their exceptionally large size and correspondingly high cost dictated that individual boats were owned by longshore men organised in groups known as 'Companies'. These Companies had their headquarters and tall wooden look-out towers along the shoal-strewn coast of East Anglia between Winterton in Norfolk and Aldeburgh in Suffolk; here the yawls were stationed and served the huge fleets of sailing vessels working their way along the channels to and from the Thames. They rendered assistance to vessels in distress, salvaged cargoes from the sands and undertook the more routine task of ferrying out pilots and replacing lost anchors and gear. These activities were traditionally undertaken by the Companies on a competitive basis.

Such an atmosphere of competition gave rise to unusually powerful and fast boats. The restrictions imposed by the fact that they were all working from an open shelving beach meant that although they had to be large enough to punch through heavy seas their construction had to combine the strength and lightness. It is said that the biggest of the yawls, such as the *Reindeer* of 70 ft., were the largest open sailing boats in Europe. Although originally three-masted, about the middle of the nineteenth century a two-masted rig was found to be equally effective and was adopted. By that time a typical yawl was 50 ft. in length, 8 ft. beam, built with a full centre-section although of only three feet depth amidships and fitted with eight thwarts. Their steamed oak frames were closely spaced, some six inches or less apart.

When sailing, stability was maintained by bags of shingle ballast which were pitched from bilge to bilge by the crew as the yawl went about. The sheet of the foresail was never

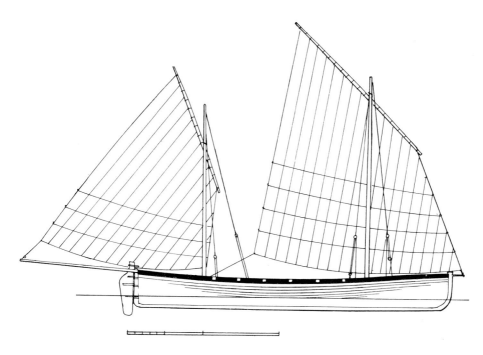

made fast but was held in the hand, with two or three turns taken round a sampson post close by the mast so that it could be quickly surged; the lives of all those aboard depended on the foresheet-man and his skill. A contemporary account of sailing a yawl gives some idea of the experience. 'I have seen the water six inches, or more, above the lee-gunnel, but only trickling in owing to the speed of the boat, although when going to windward it would be necessary to have four men bailing with buckets.' Less spectacularly the yawls were rowed in calms and oars were also shipped when sailing and it was required to assist in putting the long hull about.

A rare example of a renowned professional yacht designer, G. L. Watson, being commissioned to design a traditional work boat occurred at Lowestoft towards the end of the epoch when he planned the *Happy New Year* in 1894 and later the *Jubilee*. They proved to be fine boats, but were inferior to the best of those designed and built traditionally with the minimum of calculation. Closely-fought sailing matches between the yawls, new and old, took place as part of the annual regattas held principally at Yarmouth and Lowestoft. It was at Lowestoft that the last race for yawls was held in 1907. By that date the day of the yawl was over. Its mainstay, the great fleets of sailing vessels, were passing away either to a violent end or the breakers' yard. The final blow came when all the North Channel pilots were collected at Harwich and ships were compelled to go to one pilot station. When their days of adventure were past some yawls found a peaceful retirement as house-boats on the Broads. Others were disposed of to Clacton and Southend where they became pleasure-boats, rigged as ketches. One of the last of the yawls to remain on her home shore was the *Bittern*. Her dismantled hull, abandoned on the saltings at Southwold, survived until the nineteen thirties.

The Sheringham Crabber

The extensive off-shore banks of clean sand and rock deposited along the north Norfolk coast produce ideal conditions for a variety of crustacea, notably crabs. The craft used by the fishermen who work the grounds are simple shore-boats that have remained unchanged in hull form since at least 1829 when E. W. Cooke, the marine artist, recorded them with his usual meticulous eye for detail. The crabbers' shape and construction probably dates from a much earlier time than this; they were indeed a reminder of how our open fishing boats appeared as long ago as the Middle Ages, for they were locked in a situation where development was almost impossible.

The crabbers are still in daily use by fishermen all along the coast between Wells-next-the-Sea and Mundesley, although they are now motor-driven and are recovered when they are beached by motor-driven winches. The comparative lack of harbours involves the fishermen in negotiating long stretches of sand and shallow water when beaching their boats at any time other than high-water. This difficulty was overcome, in the days of sail, by carrying the boats bodily across the flats. Oars were passed right through opposite oar-ports (known as 'orrucks') cut in the topmost strake, of which there were three on either side. The stout ash oars were then used as handles for lifting. This process imposed severe limitations upon the size and weight of the crabbers and meant that they never grew beyond 17 ft. in length and a relatively primitive clench construction. The builders used exceptionally wide planks to form the shell of the boats, originally of oak and latterly of half-inch larch. Then as now they were brightly painted in combinations of red, white

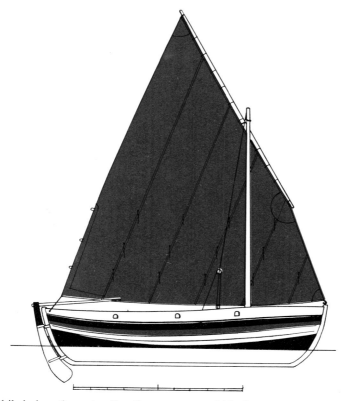

and blue, while below the water-line they were tarred black. The identical bow and stern ensured simple and therefore cheap construction; it also facilitated the setting and retrieving of the whelk and crab pots for the craft could easily be rowed in either direction. Crabbers were built by Emery of Sheringham and were particularly well thought of by the fishermen; builders also worked at Wells, Cley and Blakeney and further south at Mundesley.

In the days of sail a large dipping-lug, almost black in colour, was carried. The tack of the sail was usually made fast to the sternhead, but when running free it was secured to an iron hook on the weather side, inside the topmost strake, just forward of the mast. The sheet was never made fast when sailing but passed through a hole in the top of the stern-post and thence inboard through the after oar-port, to be held in the hand ready for freeing to cope with a heavy gust. Ballast was shipped immediately before launching and consisted of five bags of shingle. Once under way the crabbers were sailing these shifted into the weather bilge and were smartly thrown up to the windward side whenever the boat went about. On beaching the shingle was emptied out. The long rudder projected below the keel and assisted in providing the hull with some lateral grip on the water.

The north Norfolk beaches are still enlivened by the simple hulls and gay colours of the crabbers despite the fact that their numbers are sadly reduced. Periodic failures of the fishery led to groups of fishermen seeking what they trusted would be richer grounds elsewhere and leaving Norfolk. They settled along the Lincolnshire coast, at Grimsby, in Suffolk and across the Thames estuary at Whitstable. They moved together with their boats and gear, families and furniture, making the journey sensibly, if somewhat unheroically, by rail.

The Grimsby Sailing Trawler

The development of the port of Grimsby on the Humber is an example of Victorian energy and single-mindedness. The nearby port of Hull was 25 miles further from the sea and the fishermen given too low a priority for any development to be undertaken there and so the village of Grimsby was selected to rise within a few years and become a town based upon deep-sea fishing. The railway provided fine dock facilities, dug out from the marshes, and access to untapped markets at especially cheap rates, while the Dogger Bank supplied the fish. From owning one small boat in 1858 Grimsby grew to muster 815 sailing trawlers of the finest type and 15 steam trawlers, only twenty years later.

While the railway kings of the Midlands developed the port facilities, the trawlermen of Devon and Essex founded the fishery. The Brixham men had often landed fish at Scarborough, but now they had a port with unrivalled facilities at which to settle – facilities which also drew owners from Hull and Barking in Essex. The cutter-rig was the traditional one used for smacks hailing from the Humber. From the 1880's onward the ketch-rig with its smaller, more manageable, mainsail was used. The Grimsby trawlers were the largest of all the sailing fishing craft on the coast, between 70 and 80 tons, over 80 ft. in length, with a 20 ft. beam; at least one was of 100 tons. They tended to have a bluffer bow than their West Country counterparts and were considered to have a working

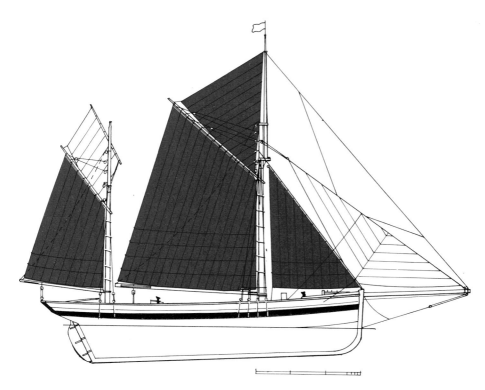

life of about 20 years. They were built at widely differing ports beside Grimsby, Brixham in Devon, Rye in Sussex, Barking on the Thames and even Elmshorn and Altona on the Elbe.

The cod smacks, besides providing accommodation in their holds for salted fish, had wet-wells in which live fish could be brought to market. It consisted of a watertight lower section of the hold connected with the sea by means of lead pipes one inch in diameter and communicating with the deck by means of a wooden trunk. Cod were caught by lines and when hauled up had their swim bladders punctured and they were then consigned by way of a hatch to the sea water circulating in the wet-well. On reaching port the smack would be able to sell live cod at a good market price or transfer them to floating boxes to await a rising market. All the smacks carried a heavily-built 16 ft. row boat on deck which was used to ferry boxed-up fish to the steam carriers that met the fleets on the fishing grounds and then loaded their catch for transhipment to market. It was an exacting and dangerous task, but injury or death by drowning were the common lot of a smacksman. Grimsby had a particularly bad name in this respect for its rapid growth produced a shortage of skilled hands and there was an absence of the family ties ashore which elsewhere did something to soften the harshness of the life.

The day of the sailing trawler at Grimsby ended nearly as suddenly as it had begun. By the first decade of the twentieth century they had been almost entirely replaced by steam and the sailing craft had gone to either a watery grave, the breakers' yard or to be sold to ports where conditions still gave sail an opportunity to show a modest profit. Half a century later there were still a score or more working for Scandinavian and Faroese owners. Some became coasters, their holds stripped out, bought for a tenth of their original cost a few years before.

The Billy Boy

The line drawn between the heavier Humber sloops and the craft known the length of the East Coast as a billy boy, was a narrow one. It might be said that if a sloop was permitted by its owners the luxury of a compass, charts and a lead line, it became a billy boy. But generally speaking the billy boy, built a century ago, was a characterful little craft, clencher built, just as the earlier keels were, with a good sheer and rigged either as a cutter or a ketch; the important difference was the bulwarks with which they were fitted. The bigger examples, which could load 120 tons of cargo, were said to be the largest clencher built craft in Europe. Knottingley, far up the river Aire in Yorkshire, was the building place of many, where there were four shipyards launching wooden ships. Billy boys were also built at Howden and at Burton upon Stather.

The mast was stepped in a tabernacle in the smaller billy boys and enabled the mast to be lowered for canal work and to deliver cargoes above bridges when trading to the Thames. The larger ones, some of which were rigged with square topsails and topgallants, had no such arrangement and their limit on the Humber was the old Barge Dock, at the inland coal port of Goole.

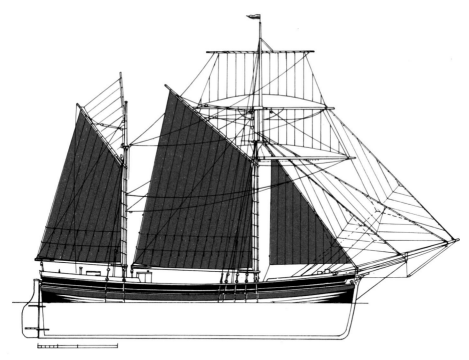

All but the largest billy boys were equipped with lee boards operated by winches. As they had rounded bilges combined with a flat floor to allow them to sit upright in a berth that dried out, some assistance to windward sailing was necessary. Square topsails had been abandoned by the early years of the twentieth century, but when the wind was abaft the beam mast they contrived to set a squaresail on a foreyard, hoisted aloft by the foresail halliards. Some even managed to set a raffee topsail above it to get the most of a fair wind when making the long haul down Channel. A typical round voyage would be to load coal for Plymouth, return with china clay from Cornwall to the Thames and then sail for the Humber with cement. Sometimes a voyage was made with shingle ballast, for unlike the spritsail barges the billy boys could not sail with an empty hold, but its sale, although showing the skipper a meagre profit, was enough to 'fill the grub locker'.

The appearance of the traditional Yorkshire billy boy was even considered old-fashioned by contemporary seafarers. The apple-bowed hull was set-off by a wale of scraped and varnished oak between rubbing strakes of red, while the bulwarks were frequently green (blue if the skipper or owner had died within the twelvemonth). Bow rails and stern quarter boards were white and the deck was tarred and sanded to ensure a firm foothold. Forward an old-fashioned handspike windlass had the traditional lucky horse-shoe nailed to the pawl-post while the forecastle and cabin chimneys were of brass-bound wood and were removable for canal work. The mast tabernacle was fitted with winches for sweating up the halliards while a dolly winch for cargo work fitted between the mast and the main-hatch. The crosstrees hinged and so saved the risk of damage. The last years of the nineteenth century saw round-sterned coasters built and referred to as billy boys, although they were constructed of steel, sailing from the Humber. But they all shared the flat sides and strongly built floors required for beach work when a skipper would put his vessel on the shore and then discharge the coal cargo into carts as the tide ebbed by means of the long-suffering crew working on the dolly-winch.

The Humber Keel

The complex pattern of rivers and canals which eventually connect with the Humber was navigated until recently by the square-sailed keel. The size of the keels was limited by the dimensions of the canal locks and the available depth of water in the natural or man-made waterways. There were Sheffield size, Manvers size, and Driffield size keels. A Sheffield keel would be 60 ft. long, 15 ft. 3 in. in beam and draw seven feet, loading 100 tons of cargo; those that worked to Lincoln could not be more than five feet deep. The Trent 'catches' were given a wider foot to the mainsail, to provide more power and no doubt due to their longer length, 75 ft., many set a mizzen lugsail. A 70 ft. keel would load as much as 170 tons of coal.

Their archaic form and rig were dictated by the canal locks through which they had to pass and their employment in two contrasting watery worlds – rural canals on one hand and the wide sand-strewn estuary of the Humber on the other. The straight sides of the hull, the very bluff bow, and the rounded stern ensured the greatest carrying capacity that could be contained in the lock-pits. The mast carried a squaresail with a brailing line, lashed to a yard and above it a topsail. Very occasionally a keel set a topgallant as well. The two-man crew of a keel needed all the mechanical assistance that could be provided in order to manage their craft when it was under sail. There were winches for handling the sheets of the sail, another pair for the tacks, one for heaving up the sail and yard, and two for managing the lee boards.

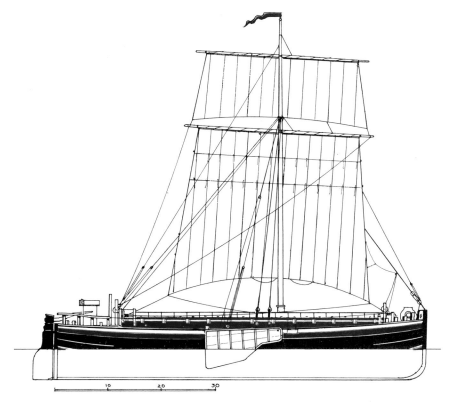

Anchor work was an essential part of the seamanship aboard the keels and a heavy anchor, with 30 fathoms of chain, was hove up by a heavy handspike windlass fitted across the bows. The square sail survived largely because it enabled a keel to sail astonishingly close to the wind and could nevertheless be easily dismantled when a keel was towed about the canals and under the bridges. When sailing hard the lee rigging could be unhooked so that the sail could be set flatter and the bowline hauled taut. The three shrouds were set up with deadeyes, heart-shaped. This shape stood up better than the normal circular variety to the frequent unshipping of the shrouds.

Many skippers owned or part-owned their vessels, lived aboard with their families, fixed their own freights with merchants, and assisted in unloading and loading. They maintained their keels at slack times, scraping the masts, tarring the hull and painting the fittings. At the stern the alternate timber heads were brought up and capped with a rail, while at the stem they projected above the deck and formed mooring posts. These were scraped and varnished, brightly painted and attractively lined in colour. An iron tiller, capable of being put hard over to enable the rudder to take up as little space as possible, was shipped for the canals. Normally a wooden one, embellished with carving and paint, was fitted.

Keels were man enough to make modest coastwise voyages, although this was really work for which their contemporaries, the Humber sloops were better adapted. At least one keel reached London and they were regularly seen at Scarborough and southward to the ports of the Wash. The last keel in work was the *Nar*, which was converted to power in 1941. Many steel keels were launched with a similar hull-form to the wooden ones, one, the *Comrade*, will, it is hoped, be fully fitted out and used for exhibitions of historical material associated with the waterways, and educational projects.

The Humber Sloop

The Humber sloop was built to the same massive form as the keel except that the sloops had a rather finer run aft in their lines and were rigged in a different style. The sloops had their own regatta, held at Boston-on-the-Humber, and the last took place as late as 1929; the final keel race was sailed in 1903.

The sloop was a much easier craft to handle in the tideway and would turn to windward in the narrow lower reaches of the Ouse or Trent at low water. The gaff mainsail was sheeted through two enormous blocks and secured just forward of the helmsman. The foresail was fitted with a boom and travelled across an iron horse; the job of the mate working the bowline when going about was likely to be a wet one as the bluff bows of a sloop threw salt spray halfway up the mast, but it was far less complicated than winding in a keel with its primitive square sail.

The fastest sloops were the ones that were built to negotiate the Market Weighton canal, on the Humber, above Hull. They were about 65 ft. overall and just under 15 ft. in beam. Some of these canal voyagers put their mast, gaff and boom ashore and blew about the waterways with a modest square sail set on a derrick pole serving as a mast. Their full equipment would be replaced when they once again entered the wider reaches of the estuary. Dredging for sand was a traditional occupation of the sloops and their crews, an alternative to sailing cargoes of sugar-beet, oil-cake, and bricks. A leather bag was

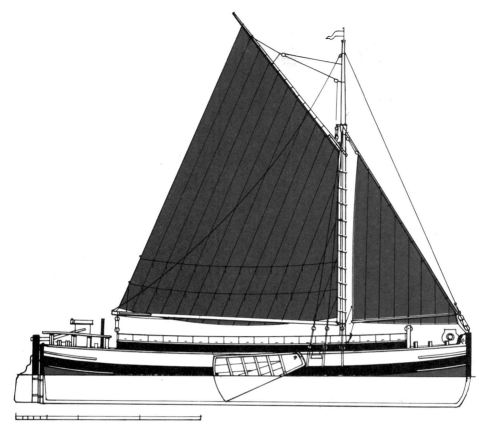

fastened to a pole and the mouth of the bag was shod with iron. The primitive contraption was suspended from a chain sling and worked along the river bottom with the aid of a winch as the sloop lay at anchor. At the mouth of the Humber a gravel bed extends from Spurn Point. This was worked by sloops going aground as the tide ebbed and then digging out the gravel and heaving it aboard and into the hold through small apertures in the deck which were secured by hatches and bolted home before setting sail. Cargoes were unloaded by a derrick roped to the foot of the mast and worked by a hand-operated dolly winch at the fore end of the hatch.

Some sloops had a single long hatch like the keels. Others, particularly the largest steel ones, had a deck for the mast, dividing the hatch into two. Like the keels, they carried lee boards and it was said the keels handled best when they were loaded slightly down by the head. The mainsail was hoisted by winches on either side of the mast. Originally the sloops had a rather flat peak to their mainsail, but latterly it became higher and doubtless set better for windward work. The sails were dressed with a mixture of horse fat and cutch. The biggest sloops, particularly those trading to the ports on the Wash and loading nearly 200 tons, carried a full cutter rig with topmast and three headsails set on a bowsprit that could be hinged upwards when in a crowded dock. Many of the sloops fitted a short bowsprit for a single jib hanked to a wire stay and set a yard topsail.

There were still a score or more sloops working at the outbreak of the Second World War. The last was the steel *Sprite*, built in 1910; she was unrigged in 1950 and converted into a lighter.

The Coble

Cobles, pronounced 'cobble' if you are a Yorkshireman, are the most distinctive of Britain's beach-boats. They were, and in some cases still are, employed on the coast from the Tweed to the Humber. Each village down the precipitous coast had its fishing fleet of cobles, varying in size and having developed individual characteristics to suit the immediate locality.

A coble, large or small, was built around an oak centre plank called the ram; this was formed from a baulk of timber with an adze, and was flat at the stern and then gradually changed in section until it was narrow and deep. The ram was carried forward by the swath-piece to a deep forefoot. The stem and deadwood were then fitted at the bow, with a narrower 'stomach piece' inside it, the difference in the thickness providing a rabbet for fixing the plankends. The planks are referred to as 'strokes' along the North East Coast and the garboard strokes, the planks nearest the ram plank, are known as the 'sand-strokes'. These are fitted next, to be followed by further wide strokes of larch, fastened with copper nails closed over roves and all brought together at the stern to give a very pronounced trumble-home. It is only at this stage that the timbers are fitted, notched so that they fit neatly over the inner overlapping strokes. Originally smaller cobles were built with only three strokes between the sandstroke and the gunwale, but this has gradually

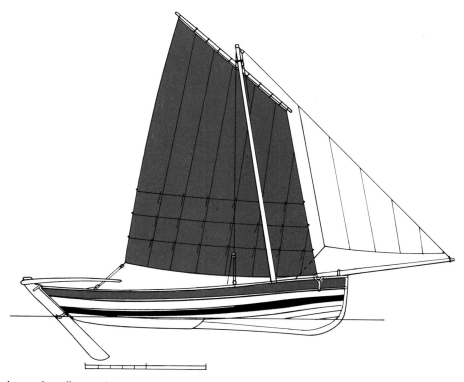

changed until a modern motor-coble has as many as seven. The short side-keels aft are called draft keels because these bore the brunt of the wear as a coble was drawn up the landings, as the beaches were called, stern first. At Staithes, this was done by hand, using the long oars as skids.

Depending upon the size and the demands of the work in which it would be employed, the position of the thofts, as the thwarts were called, varied. The smaller cobles, between Scarborough and Robin Hoods Bay had four fixed thofts, in the foremost one of which was stepped the mast. The fifth, forward of the steering thoft, could be removed to make room for nets.

The cobles varied considerably in size and shape. Those which lay at moorings could be given a deeper forefoot to afford a good grip of the water when going to windward. All had a very deep rudder, projecting well below the keel to assist in sailing close to the wind. Pilot cobles tended to be narrower and were painted black, unlike the fishing cobles which were painted blue, white and red. All cobles carried shingle ballast in bags which were moved to the weather bilge; salmon cobles, small and light, were up to about 24 ft. long, those used for the winter long-lining were 26 to 28 ft. overall, while the 'ploshers' were used for the herring fishing, decked and ranged up to 35 ft. and even 40 ft. in length.

Large sharp-sterned cobles, called mules, were built for the herring drifting and for pleasure sailing with summer visitors. They set a narrow dipping lug, with at least three rows of reef-points and the bigger ones carried a foresail on a bowsprit and occasionally a shorter mizzen-mast. The sailing of a coble needed especial skills and the main sheet was never made fast; a bowline kept the luff of the mainsail taut on the wind and the tack lead through an eye on the weather bow or hooked to a wire horse in eyes of coble secured through holes in the gunwale.

The Yorkshire Yawl

The harbours of Whitby and Scarborough were substantial places of refuge, paid for largely by dues levied on the coal fleets and developed in the first half of the nineteenth century. They enabled a fleet of at least one hundred yawls to be established there. The Yorkshire yawls were large clench-built craft with heavy bows, between 50 and 60 ft. long and were originally lugsail-rigged, with the distinctive feature of a mizzen topmast. Their sheerline was reminiscent of the cobles and gave a pleasing wave-like profile to the hull, ending in a lute stern. The first of the yawls had originated at a time before trawling had become common on the North East Coast and ground fish were caught by hook and line in various ways. Just as the Lowestoft drifters changed from lug-rig to fore and aft sails in the seventies and eighties, so did the Yorkshire yawls. They set a loose-footed mainsail sheeted on a heavy iron horse crossing the full width of the deck, just forward of the mizzen mast. While they followed the East Anglian drifters in changing their rig, they never quite set the same variety and quality of fine-weather canvas at sea. The yawls fitted out and commenced long-line fishing in February; this continued until July and they took ice with them to the grounds in an attempt to preserve the catch. In August the herring nets were brought out of store and loaded aboard. The drift-netting went on until the end of November when, very sensibly, the boats were laid-up for the months when the mood of the North Sea was at its worst.

A tall wooden capstan was fitted aft of the fish hold to haul in the nets. Wooden treads were nailed to the deck to assist the men who manned the capstan bars to keep their footing on the swaying decks, slippery with fish-slime. Capstan hands were not regular

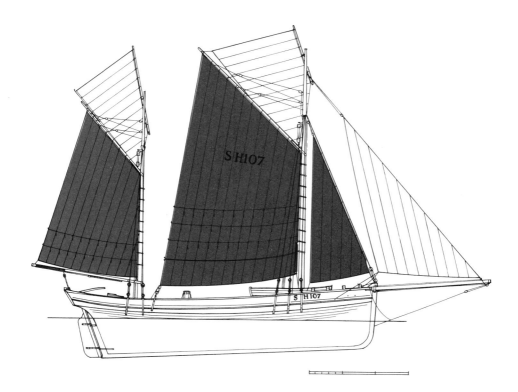

seamen but three or four casuals, often picked up at the pier-head. They and the crew lived in a dark cabin in the stern where there were six berths augmented by a deep shelf beneath the after deck (and the tramp of the helmsman's feet) where the boys slept. Food was eaten and sleep snatched between hauling the nets. There was no table of any size and a deep tin plate was wedged on the fisherman's lap while he sat on the lockers to eat. The food was usually fried fish and prepared by the cook who was all too often the most recently recruited member of the crew. Tea was brewed in a large kettle to which was added sugar and condensed milk and remained unemptied until the tea-leaves reached the level of the lid.

A small coble was carried on deck, to starboard of the foremast. It was launched at sea, through a removable gate in the bulwarks, to net small herring for bait when long-lining. Each yawl fished with about 120 nets for herring, each net 60 yds. long. The nets were cleared of fish as they came aboard at sea and the herring were shovelled into the well, as the hold was called, and then the nets would be shot again. When they grew older the clench-built yawls were given another skin by doubling. This was done by filling in the lands with feather-edged boards and then covering the whole hull with another carvel skin, while iron knees strengthened the fabric within. When this was completed it enabled the old yawls to survive until the day when the steam drifters finally replaced them.

The Scottish Scaffie

The scaffie, variously known as a scaffa or scaith, was the boat native to the Scottish East Coast, particularly the harbours and shores north of Rattray Head. It was the type from which others later developed, when during the second half of the nineteenth century improved communications encouraged a vast expansion of the fishing industry. The scaffie's general form, although it varied in size, derived from the Viking tradition of a double-ended clench-built open boat, constructed as a light shell and then strengthened by the insertion of frames or shaped timbers and thwarts. Between Wick in the north and Buckie the scaffie continued to be built until the twentieth century.

The earliest scaffies were built on a keel of some 30 ft. and their curved stem and stern post, raking at 45 degrees gave them an overall length of over 40 ft., with a beam of 13 ft. They were lightly constructed of wide larch planks, and despite their relatively large size were without decks, partly to keep their weight down to a level to enable them to be easily hauled ashore at the end of the fishing season. Their maximum beam was well aft of amidships and the clench construction naturally produced hollow bowlines. The early scaffies were quite open and, no doubt in the expert hands of fishermen, they behaved well enough and rowed easily on calms. Problems arose when, as was the custom, temporary hands were shipped during the busy herring season. An inexperienced crew scrambling

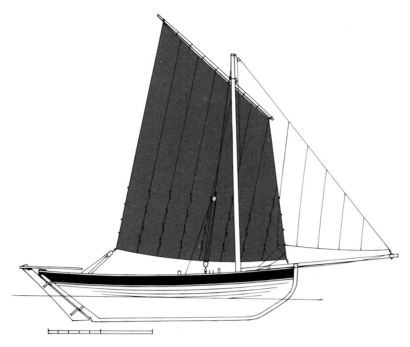

for the sail as she went about in conditions of a heavy sea, rapidly losing way, was instrumental in causing many losses; at the best of times their short keel made them unweatherly craft. The owners were reluctant to deck the boats as this would be both expensive and limit the accommodation for nets and stowing the catch, while increasing the height of the sides would make hauling in the nets more difficult. However, with some official encouragement and the admirably practical encouragement from the R.N.L.I., who built and worked an improved scaffie, the fishermen gradually accepted the change to a safer, more weatherly vessel for their work at sea. The essential improvement was a fitted deck, somewhat below the gunwale, to enable oars to be shipped and a long central hatchway which could be covered with hatch-boards and a tarpaulin cloth in bad weather. Not only were new scaffies launched combining the new modifications, but old ones were lengthened amidships and decked in.

Fleets of scaffies, numbering over one thousand, went to the great summer fishing at Wick in the far north, many of the boats manned by crofters as sea-going labourers whose job it was to heave in the nets. The increased profits from the expanding industry were used to purchase better, more seaworthy boats, and gradually the zulu (q.v.) replaced the older scaffie. The last big scaffies were rigged with a foremast in the bow and another, only slightly shorter, a little aft of amidships; an iron winch was now fitted for hauling in the nets.

Groups sailed north to the Shetlands and the Hebrides and in the eighteen sixties the custom of going south to the East Anglian Autumn fishery had begun. In three-masted scaffies the nets were shot from the starboard side and when all were out the foremast was lowered into a crutch, the mizzen unshipped, the rudder brought on deck and the boat laid to her nets; at dawn they were brought in over the stern.

The smaller scaffies were known as yawls, an echo perhaps of the name of the Orkney yole rather than any reference to their rig, and today just one small example of these remains under sail, the little *Seaspray* at Stonehaven.

The Scottish Zulu

Tradition has it that in 1879 a boat-builder of Lossiemouth on the Moray Firth combined the straight bow of the fifie with the long raking stern of the older scaffie and produced a fishing craft which had the finer characteristics of both types. The deep forefoot gave it a good grip upon the water for working to windward while the stern post, raking at 45 degrees or more, lengthened the waterline and gave a clean run aft. The new type became called 'zulus' to commemorate the successful conclusion of the current colonial war in Africa. The zulus retained the traditional clench construction until 1885 when carvel building was introduced. The craft for the herring fishery were growing in size every year; the last of the zulus built with the traditional clencher method were 40 ft. on the keel, but with the adoption of carvel construction the length of hull could be increased until boats were 75 ft. overall. The substitution of the hand-operated capstan by the steam capstan enabled nets, sails and anchors to he handled mechanically.

These great craft were built with beech keels, oaken stem and sternposts and the frames were usually of oak, although larch was used occasionally, while the beams were of Scotch fir. The sheer line rose considerably to a powerful bow and was accentuated by three iron-shod rubbing strakes.

The enormously strong foremast was unsupported by any standing rigging, only the halliards and burton. The masts were of Norwegian whitewood and it was quite usual for a spar-maker to trim a mast from a two-foot square, 60 ft. long baulk of timber. When fishing

the main mast lowered into a substantial crutch alongside the mizzen mast. The great lug-sails were hoisted with treble-sheave blocks. The foresail tack was hooked to the stemhead and there were three eyes placed at varying distances inboard from the bow, to be used when the sail was reefed. A chain secured the tack of the standing lug mizzen to the foot of the mizzen mast while its foot was extended beyond the stern by an outrigger. A long bowsprit, of herculean girth, was set through a gammon iron, well to starboard of the stemhead and its heel was housed close to the main mast. The mainsail carried no less than six rows of reef-points. When making short tacks the sail was set 'a'monk' so that the frequent re-setting of the sail to the leeward side of the mast on each tack was avoided. This meant that tack of the sail was taken to the foot of the mast and although it did not set so well it saved a prodigious amount of work. The zulus were at first steered by a tiller, but wheels were soon adopted and were set horizontally in the extreme stern.

It might well be asked why such an unsophisticated sail plan was retained and developed on such a huge scale. No doubt native conservatism played its part, but nevertheless it did have certain advantages. The absence of rigging was a real benefit when fishing for there was little to entangle the nets; packed into small harbours during the fishing season the less rigging there was to snarl up with one's neighbours the better. As large crews, eight or nine at least, were shipped for the fishing there was no incentive to modify the sail plan so that it could be worked more economically with fewer hands. But the day of these magnificent luggers passed rapidly away with the introduction of motors, shortly before the First World War. Many were fitted with engines, a few changed to gaff rig and some became coasters carrying cargoes. The last, the *Muirneag,* built at Buckie in 1903, was broken up in 1947.

The Scottish Fifie

Due perhaps to their geographical proximity to the differing boat-building tradition of England, the fishing craft of Fife showed less affinity to that of Scandinavia than those craft north of the Moray Firth. Until about 1855 all fifies, as the fishing boats built between Eyemouth and Aberdeen were known, were entirely undecked, double ended, but with a deeper keel, more heavily built than the scaffies and the stem and stern post were almost vertical. The lines fore and aft were comparatively sharp, while they had a full section amidships enabling them to take the ground, of steep floors. The majority were clench-built and only later, when they increased in size, carvel-built. The rig consisted of a high dipping lug-sail forward and a smaller standing lug-sail aft.

All the fifies engaged in the herring fishery, at first in the northern summer netting, then at Scarborough and finally to the southward at Yarmouth and Lowestoft where some were actually owned. Hartlepool was really their southerly limit. In winter herring could be caught in the Firth of Forth and many fifies and their sister craft the zulus (q.v.) went long-lining. Some made their way through the locks of the Caledonian Canal and fished in the Irish Sea, landing catches at the Isle of Man. While they never reached the length of the huge zulus, fifies were commonly 65 ft. long, with a 7 ft. 6 in. depth of hold and a beam of 20 ft. The timber used in their construction was either Scottish oak or larch; American elm was used for the keel and gunwale while oak was cut for the stem and sternposts.

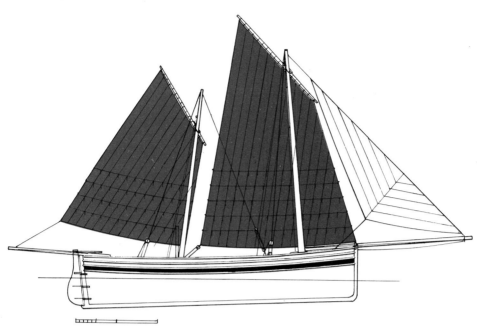

At one time the fifies had a boom (the word 'boom' in Scotland is applied to any outrigged spar, either jigger-boom over the stern or bowsprit) but latterly this was rarely set and a jib was only carried in fine weather. The entrance to the net and fish-holds was from a large hatch amidships and beneath the hold was carried up to 20 tons of stone ballast. The timber heads, as in most decked Scottish fishing boats in the days of sail, were brought up above deck level some 17 ins. and planked externally to provide a continuous low rail round the hull. It must have been an arrangement which one can only consider to have been fraught with danger for the crew. However, factors in favour of safety on deck were often in conflict with the easiest way to work fishing gear and no doubt the low rail assisted in bringing in the loaded nets. The helmsman sat on a stump of timber as he steered the vessel from a horizontal wheel. A 12 h.p. steam capstan was carried on deck, aft of the mizzen mast. When entering a crowded harbour under sail a lugger carried, ready on deck, two canvas drogues, known as 'fly anchors' and these were towed over-side on each quarter, made fast on cleats to slow the craft down.

Smack-rigged fifies were quite common. The smack-rigged vessels had a considerable vogue on the east coast of Aberdeenshire between 1870–80, but then the fishermen reverted to the older lug-sail. Once again, at the end of sail gaff-rigged fifies were seen. Some of these were auxiliaries for it was found, a few years before the First World War, that by fitting an engine the wooden fifies could compete with the steam drifters. But their days were numbered and their passing was hastened by the immensely changed conditions in the herring fishing in the world of 1919. Like the zulus, a number were employed as coasting craft.

The Shetland Sixareen

The Shetland sixareen has long since ceased fishing – the last of them lie split and wrung on the beaches of our most northerly isles. But its interest is in the fact that it preserves in its build and rig elements of the Viking tradition and the part it played in a social organisation which, although it lasted until the end of the nineteenth century, belonged to a medieval way of life. The Shetland Isles are barren and without timber, but the seas around them are rich in fish. The sixareen was built to fish amongst the islands and so far afield that their crews could be within sight of Norway.

Until the 1830's boats were imported from Norway in pieces, ready formed to be put together; after that date only timber and boards were imported and the sixareen dates from that time. The sixareen was used for the 'haaf' or deepsea fishery. With crews of six they sailed or rowed to the distant fishing banks for cod and ling, mainly on the edge of the Continental Shelf in spring and summer and were at sea for several days if the weather remained fine. This was the most important fishery to the Shetlanders and the sixareen was developed especially for it.

The summer fishing was centred on the 'haaf' stations, established on various points around the islands and the boats had moorings in sheltered bays while the men lived in primitive stone huts ashore. The sixareens were rowed or sailed to the fishing grounds and set long-lines carrying 1,200 hooks – a good haul would represent one and a half ton of fish and this would load a boat to her limits. Sixareens set out with stone ballast to stiffen them, which was jettisoned as the weight of the catch mounted. On reaching the station the catch was landed, cleaned, washed and salted, then dried in the wind and sun.

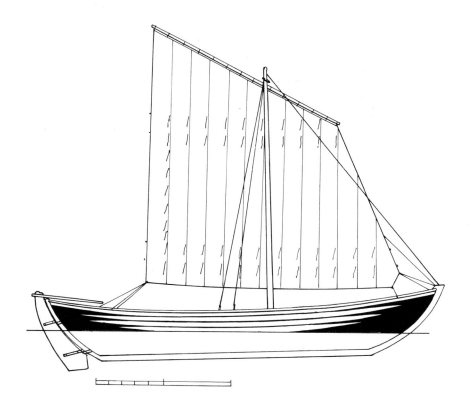

A sixareen of, say, the eighteen eighties, was 37 ft. overall, the length of keel 23 ft. and breadth 8½ ft. It was built of oak frames and larch planks – larch that was not allowed to season so that it was easier to shape. The sixareens were built as lightly as possible to enable them to be rowed easily, and they were not expected to last more than seven years. After that time they were broken up and a much smaller 'eela' constructed from the salvaged material. They were fastened with hand-wrought iron nails as it was considered they did not draw, or stretch, as copper was liable to do. The skin was about ¾ ins. and there were about nine planks to a side. The bands, as the frames were called, were of oak and went from gunwale to gunwale, but the builders did not fix them to the keel. The sides of the craft were held together by narrow beams, above which were fitted five removable thwarts or 'tafts'. A pump was fitted aft, near the helmsman, but in an emergency bailing was done, very effectively, by a large wooden shovel. The mast was stepped almost exactly amidships and stayed with shrouds which were led well aft then through a hole in the gunwale and simply hitched. The forestay led through a hole in the stemhead. The main sheet was a rope attached to the sail at one end, passed through a hole in the gunwale and back through a thimble in the clew of sail, and was held by the steersman. A bowline, with a crowsfoot attached to the sail, led the forestay and down to the bow and helped to set the sail well when on the wind.

The Orkney Yole

The people of Orkney looked to crofting first and the sea second for their livelihood, for despite their proximity to the mainland the seas around the Orkneys are even more perilous than those about the more northern islands. The Orkney jol or yole did not therefore retain the characteristics of the Viking longship to the same extent as the Shetland boats. Its shape and rig was adapted to long-lining offshore for cod and ling and using the seine net or 'sweep-net' as it was known locally. They did not venture beyond offshore limits to secure a catch and acted as passage boats between the islands.

The yoles were double-ended, but like the saffies their hull-lines were full and were built with a beam – length ratio of almost two to one. Like the Shetlanders they were forced to send to Norway for boat-building materials, a trade arranged until relatively recently on a simple barter system. The yoles were constructed with ten planks between gunwale and the keel, clencher fashion fixed with galvanised nails on to sawn oak frames, notched over the planks. An average yole would be built on a 14 ft. keel, but her curving bow and raked stempost produced an overall length of 19 ft. and a hull which had flaring bows and quarters. A passage boat, connecting the islands and carrying cargo and passengers might load as much as two tons; a cargo that might include sheep, paraffin, oatmeal and whisky.

Unlike the long and lean sixareen, the yole was primarily a sailing craft, showing unmistakable signs of the Orkneys' closer contacts with the Scottish mainland. The boats from Westeray in the North of the group, were rigged with two masts, almost identical in

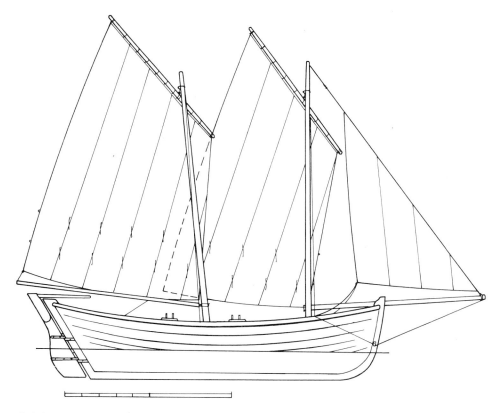

height, the after one raking noticeably towards the stern. On each was rigged a standing lug-sail, with two rows of reef-points; the foot of the after-sail was usually extended with a boom fitted with a gooseneck. A bowsprit was set on which was carried a single foresail, set without a forestay. The Southern Orkney yole was rigged somewhat differently to her more northern sister and carried two spritsails, with the sprits rigged on alternate sides of the sail. It is an unusual arrangement for the far north and it is possible that it might have been adopted during the eighteenth century in imitation of large merchantmen's boats or whale-boats. The Orkneys were favourite places for the recruitment of crews in the days of sail.

The bowsprit on both types of rig passed through a gammon iron on the port side of the stemhead and its heel was fixed in another iron on the foremast. The preference for a bowsprit to be carried on either port or starboard of the stem varied but one side was strictly adhere to within a clearly defined length of coast. It was perhaps chosen in deference to the prevailing wind for a jib is dropped to leeward and is better handled if it is normally to leeward of the stemhead. Whatever the reason, East Coasters carry their bowsprit to starboard and Scottish vessels to port as do the West Countrymen.

Two pairs of oars were worked on the yoles in calms and were fitted between double thwole pins – another feature which distinguishes them from the sixareens which had a single thwole pin and the oar was held in place by a wide grommet or 'humbaband'. The latter allowed the oar to be brought inboard rapidly and lie secure, ready for immediate use. The yoles were largely replaced by the larger and more powerfully-built fifies from the mainland and those that remained were fitted with motors.

The Loch Fyne Skiff

Loch Fyne, close by the Firth of Clyde, has always been noted for the fine quality of its herring. They kept the smoke-houses in the little harbours busy and a large fleet of drift-net boats hard at work all about the sea lochs. Campbeltown, as well as Tarbert, were filled with craft, largely herring drifters, but also finding employment working the prolific Ballantrae banks, the haunt of fine cod and turbot. These were caught by long-line; the catches were landed at nearby Girvan. In the eighteen eighties gaff-rigged smacks were introduced, a rig rarely met with on the coast of Scotland in use aboard fishing boats. They were about 30 ft. overall with a deep draught and were also exceptional in having a broad transom stern which raked well aft, giving a relatively short length of keel. The classification of Scottish fishing boats for the payment of dues etc. was by length of keel so that the increase of deck space provided by a raked bow or stern was an advantage.

From 1822 the Caledonian Canal allowed the passage of vessels from the East Coast, where fishing techniques and boat-building were more highly developed, to the West of Scotland. This brought an influence which profoundly affected West Coast boats and, generally speaking, they tended to derive from examples of the smaller craft on Scotland's other coastline. The final development of the sailing fishing boat on the Firth of Clyde was the Loch Fyne skiff. Although its profile, with its deep keel aft and a steeply-raked stern-post, was very similar to the East Coast zulu, they were always referred to as skiffs

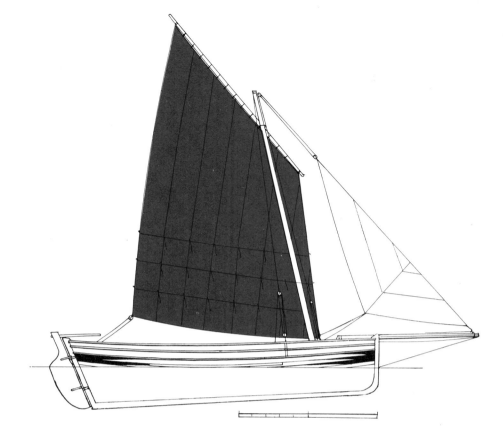

and reached their highest point in numbers in the decade immediately before the First World War. They were open except for a short foredeck, beneath which was a cabin, with less than five feet of head-room, fitted with berths and a stove. The hulls were at first clencher-built, but later carvel; the topsides were of pitchpine and were varnished to enhance its attractive grain and display the quality of the builders' workmanship. The skiffs were lightly built, although up to 35 ft. in length, with a beam of 10 ft. and drawing six feet aft. The relatively light construction was encouraged by the fact that on days when the breeze fell away the crews had to labour at the 20 ft. oars to bring a catch home. On such occasions it was possible to lighten the boats further by jettisoning some of the internal stone ballast. It was important that they should be able to sail swiftly and seek shelter (for the area they fished was well provided with harbours) than to battle out a storm. Moreover, unlike other Scottish work-boats, they took the opportunity to sail for sport. Many of their crews had seen some service as paid hands aboard the Clyde-based yachts and had acquired a taste for sailing to win. Competition to have a boat which would carry off regatta prizes in races for fishing boats, if not openly admitted, was keen.

A mizzen mast for the Loch Fyne herring boats had been tried and rejected. The last of the sailing skiffs set a single tall standing lug on a mast stepped in the bow and steeply raked aft. There was provision in the mast-step for the heel to be progressively increased as the sail was reefed so that the centre of effort remained approximately in the same position; the sail had four rows of reef-points. A bowsprit was carried and projected about 10 ft. beyond the stemhead and skiffs carried three jibs, the size chosen to be set depending on the weather conditions.

The Gabbert

The name gabbert survives on the West Coast of Scotland and the Clyde even today, but it is used in a general and usually nostalgic context to refer to the small coaster of the days before steam appeared in the shape of the characterful 'puffers'. Strictly it referred only to the small craft built to traverse the restricted stretches of the Forth and Clyde Canal and which traded about the Firth of Clyde, while in summer they might even venture northwards. The whole area of sea, islands and sea lochs, if judged from the map would appear to be admirably suited to a small vessel trading under sail, but is in fact beset with treacherous tidal streams; it is open to the full force of the Atlantic swell, awe-inspiring even in the infrequent lulls between storms. Trading under sail consisted of snatching a passage between one precarious anchorage and another. The gabberts were restricted in size by the locks on the Forth and Clyde Canal; they allowed the passage of a vessel 70 ft. long overall, with a beam of 20 ft. and a draught of about 6 ft. but no more. This became the upper limit to the size of the wooden-built gabbert loading about 70 tons. The unrigged lighters on the Forth and Clyde Canal and later the smacks built especially to pass through the Canal were also known as gabberts although not strictly belonging to the same class. To cope with canal work the rig of the true gabberts was arranged to lower to deck level. They were round-sterned, without any counter in order to make as much as possible of the space provided in the lock-pits. The alternate timber-heads on the hull were brought up above deck level a foot or so and joined by a wooden rail. Fore and aft the timbers were further extended to provide a waist-high rail for the helmsman at the tiller and the crew when working the handspike barrel-windlass forward. The rig was of the simplest. Unlike

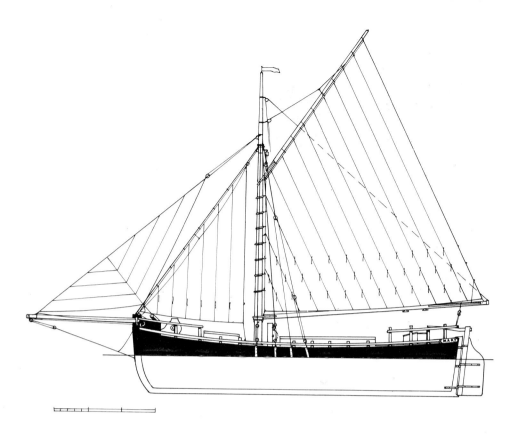

the smacks that gradually replaced them, they never carried a topmast and were provided with a simple sloop rig. Those that ventured further afield to Tarbert on Loch Fyne or a remote beach on Kintyre where the cargo would be unloaded into tumbrils, might set a bowsprit with the jib hauled out on a traveller. The gabberts were well adapted for beach work for they were strongly built and their shallow draught and flat floors gave them the ability to remain conveniently upright for discharging cargoes, but they must have been poor things to work to windward. The majority were built at Bowling and Dumbarton on the Clyde.

Trading to the Isle of Arran in the Firth of Clyde with coal and returning with malting barley was the mainstay of the gabbert in her heyday, the mid-nineteenth century. But eventually the 'puffer' drove sail from even this trade. Quite early on it was seen to be economically profitable to build very small steamers to trade amongst the Western Isles for passenger and freight rates were high, while elsewhere it was financially disastrous because of the high overheads of powered craft. The fact that nearby was the advanced steam technology of the Clyde and its shipyards, must also have affected the situation. These small steamers were known as 'puffers' and were one of the few mechanically-powered craft which have endeared themselves to a wider public in a way usually reserved for sailing ships. They even produced their own legend, recorded in popular fiction. At least the gabberts and the coastal trading smacks of the Firth of Clyde bowed out to worthy successors.

The Mersey and Weaver Flat

While the somewhat unprepossessing name flat was a vague one, it survived to identify the sailing barges plying in the Mersey and the complex pattern of industrialised waterways and canals joining with the estuary. A comprehensive network was developed in the late eighteenth century and its object was to provide access for the flats so that exports and imports could connect with Liverpool and the Mersey.

The flats were massively built with oak timbers and bow planking; the four planks at the turn of the bilge were of four-inch rock elm. The decks were of pitch-pine. Sailing flats were always carvel-built. Little of the keel projected, although longitudinal strength was provided by an unusually strong keelson and hogpiece, as much as three feet deep. The smaller flats working on the Weaver had a heavy square stern and their size was limited by the locks to an overall length of 68 ft., a depth of 6 ft. and a beam of 14 ft. They were built with one long hatch and for work on the canals a lowering mast was essential. This was not set in a tabernacle but pivoted between two massive uprights and the foot of the mast rested upon the keelson. To make the most of the space in the lock-pits the Weaver flats were built with a heavy square stern. One of these, the *Daresbury,* launched in the mid-eighteenth century, survived as a canal maintenance boat on the Weaver Navigation until the 1950's. Until the last she had at her stern a stout post, bored out for a pump and fitted with a large cleat for the mainsheet. The traditional cargoes for these flats was South

Lancashire coal, shipped from the pits to the salters along the Weaver. From the eighteen sixties onwards the Weaver became dominated by steam towage and the flats, if they were not relegated to becoming unrigged towing barges, were forced to find employment outside the canals.

There had always been bigger sharp-sterned flats which had existed contemporaneously with the square-sterned ones, now all the new flats that were built were round-sterned which improved the water-flow to the rudder when the craft were laden. These flats loaded up to 175 tons and drew as much as nine feet; they had the same high-peaked sloop rig which the older flats carried. The smaller 'inside flats' carried a crew of two and did not trade beyond the Mersey Bar light vessel; the others went much further afield. There was much warping about docks and tidal basins to be done, and all flats had a windlass with a pair of fitted crank handles. To enable the main barrel of the winch to be used for other work than raising the anchor, the cable could be hung clear of the barrel on a row of hooks suspended from an iron bar.

Once the necessity of lowering down the gear for canal work was over flats were launched with fixed masts, equipped with substantial winches at the foot for setting sails. The windlass drums, the wooden rail stanchions and the cabin hatch were all brightly painted, while the masthead above the hounds were picked out in contrasting bands of colours as the owner's distinguishing marks.

Flats had a reputation for longevity; many achieved a century of service afloat, due, it was said, to the salt cargoes they carried preserving their timbers. There were still sailing flats on the Mersey in the nineteen thirties – most of them trading between Widnes and Liverpool, but they had all passed away by the Second World War except one, the *Keskadale* and now she too has gone.

The Jigger Flat

The flats of the Mersey had always traded further afield than their limited sail-plan would indicate. It is certain that from the eighteenth century they were not only plying a river trade but most had found their way about the whole of the upper part of the Irish Sea and reached Dublin. They took coal and salt outwards from the Mersey and returned with metallic ores, quarried stone and timber. The size of the sloop-rigged flat grew and produced an even bigger mainsail; they reached nearly 80 ft. overall and the natural step of introducing the ketch rig was taken. These were known as jigger flats and appeared in the eighteen eighties.

Flats which went beyond the Mersey Bar light vessel had to carry three hands and the master to hold a certificate of competency. The bigger jigger flats shaded into becoming seagoing ketches; but none was fitted with topmasts or bowsprits and all had very large hatches in comparison with the traditional seagoing vessel. The main hatch, always a point of weakness in heavy weather, was, however, divided into two by a fixed section called 'no man's land'. The jigger flats also set a yard topsail and a little jib-topsail. The peak halliards were of chain and led to a winch at the starboard foot of the mainsail and the throat went to a winch-barrel to port; some flats also had a chain throat halliard. It was quite common for flats to have a wrought-iron rod to serve as a forestay. The foresail, on a fixed sheet and cut with a very full gore, travelled across an iron horse, foreward of the mast, called by the flatmen a 'transom'. All flats carried, or towed, a cock-boat used mainly for running out lines when mooring up, it had a full bow so that a flatman might jump into it without danger of a capsize.

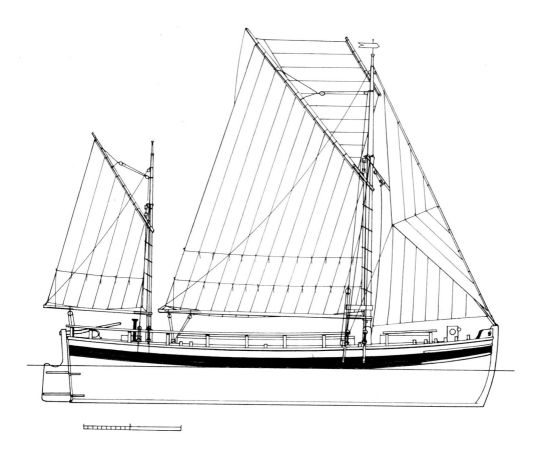

Ordinary flats had their rails along the hull in three sections. Those at the stern were fixed to the stanchions, which were about two feet high and brought up through the covering board. There was then a gap and another length between the quarters and the rigging, which was removable and the stanchions that supported it were hinged so that they could be laid fore and aft. The distance covered by the chain-plates of the main rigging, which were set flush with the topsides, was without any rail and then there was a short fixed length by the fore hatch. Between the stanchions were short timberheads and from these fenders were hung. The timberheads were given an inward cant to prevent them catching any ropes on a neighbouring craft. The rudder was fixed to the gudgeon irons in such a way that it did not unship should a flat take the ground. Some of the bigger jigger flats had built-up rails. Such a one was the *Pilot,* 80 ft. overall, with a beam of 21 ft. and a depth of hold of 8½ ft.; she was 103 tons and was the largest ever built at Northwich. Northwich was the main building centre for flats and a succession of ship-builders worked there, launching them throughout the eighteenth and nineteenth centuries. One of the last jigger flats was the *Eustace Carey,* launched in 1905 on the St. Helen's Canal. A few steel flats were built at Northwich, of enormous carrying capacity but few pretensions to good looks. The last jigger flats were the *Sarah Latham,* a Chester river flat and almost a coasting ketch built to a Barrow pattern, and the *Pilot,* a less sophisticated vessel for she had full rails added in the 'twenties. Both were by then auxiliaries.

The Liverpool Pilot Schooner

The Mersey Pilot Service began with local fishermen who combined fishing for a liveli-hood with conducting vessels in and out of the port. The fishermen's hard-won knowledge of sands and tides, shoals and deeps, qualified them for the work, but they were unlicensed and not responsible to any authority. It was not until 1738 that the first comprehensive chart of the River Mersey and Liverpool Bay was drawn up, prepared with the assistance of three of the senior pilots.

The emergence of Liverpool in the eighteenth century as a major port brought with it the regularisation of pilotage and in 1766 the Liverpool Pilotage Act was passed. In that year there were nine pilot boats, stubby little 36 ft. sloops with a beam of about one-third their length, bluff-bowed and furnished with a square tuck stern. They were built without bulwarks although there was a small cockpit aft for the helmsman and some protection was provided by wooden rails on iron supports. Later the sloops had quarter cloths of painted canvas, coloured red with a distinctive white border. The Mersey Pilot Service anticipated a modern practice by painting the topsides of their craft a bright yellow, while below the waterline the hull was treated with white lead and tallow. The tradition was strenuously fought for when, in 1832, the Customs insisted that all small craft around the coast were to be painted black to make recognition at sea more simple.

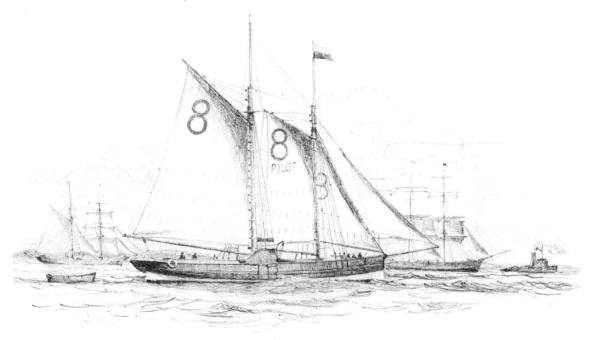

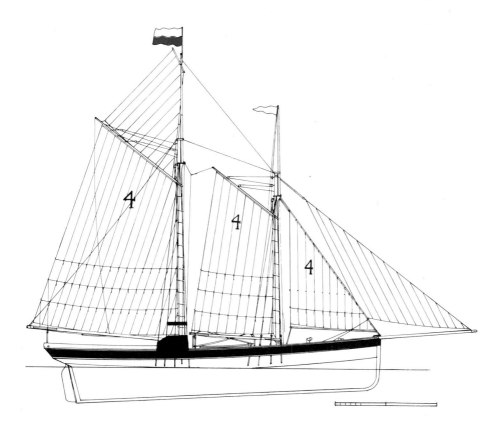

The sloops were heavily rigged in order to stand up to heavy weather; three shrouds and a runner each side supported the mast and the jib halliards were of chain. In order that the risk of damage when coming alongside could be reduced to a minimum topmasts were never carried. When not cruising in the estuary the sloops laid in Amlwen harbour, awaited homeward-bound ships. By the middle of the nineteenth century there were over a dozen active, owned chiefly by master-pilots or men retired from the Service. This arrangement proved unsatisfactory and eventually, in 1881, the Dock Board purchased and controlled all the craft on pilot duty. Some time before this change the continued growth in size of the pilot-boats, some were over 50 tons, led to the adoption of the schooner rig. The huge size of a big cutter's mainsail made it a liability when a sloop was keeping station in winter-time. The first schooner was the wooden *Pioneer,* of 53 tons, acquired in 1852; other followed rapidly and were magnificent yacht-like vessels, indeed some were designed and built by yacht builders, while one, the *Sappho,* was originally a yacht. They were some 80 ft. in length, with long keels, short counters and straight stems; at least one was built of steel. Features of the pilot schooners were canvas dodgers lashed in the main rigging and the large boarding boats they carried which were slung outboard by heavy davits amidships. The boats perpetuated the tradition of the old sloops by being painted yellow and were used to put pilots aboard ships. The *George Holt,* of 78 tons, built in 1892 at Dartmouth, was the last of the sailing schooners acquired by the Service. In 1896 the first screw steamer was introduced and rapidly replaced the schooners, and the last, the *George Holt,* was sold in 1904. At nearby Fleetwood the pilots also favoured schooners and the last they owned was the *Falcon*; she was sold out of the pilot service in 1919 and she is still sailing on the Clyde.

The Morecambe Bay Prawner

The purpose of these shapely craft was to supply potted shrimps for the high-tea tables of West Lancashire. A prosaic calling perhaps, but to work the channels and gullies of Morecambe Bay required a craft that could turn in its own length, work well to windward and lie-to with a docility that enabled its two-man crew to sort out the benison provided by the trawl.

The earlier boats had a conventional long, straight keel and bow, combined with a counter stern. To sail these heavy craft a full cutter rig with a tall topmast was essential. Before the turn of the century, largely due to the enterprise of Crossfield at Arnside and Armour at Fleetwood a new hull developed. The profile became more yachtlike, with a cutaway stem, a rounded forefoot flowing into a curved keel finishing at a steeply raking sternpost – a change in shape which made the prawners very quick on the helm. The garboards were hollow and the bilges well rounded while the sheerline came down low to a rounded counter so that the trawl could be brought aboard easily.

The prawners were of broadly three sizes. The smallest were about 25 ft. overall and did not have their decking brought aft of the mast. Others, the biggest of which were 35 ft. overall, had a beam of 9 ft. and drew 5 ft. aft; their section amidships was sufficiently full

to enable them to take the ground at low water without risk of filling as the tide made. On a short pole mast, supported with three shrouds a side, set up with deadeyes, a well peaked-up mainsail was carried. Above this was a topsail carried on a long yard, the heavy bowsprit ran out-board through a gammon iron on the stemhead and was set without a bobstay, which might foul the fishing gear.

Lancashire prawners, or nobbies as they were sometimes called, did not often do more than work a tide and then return to port. There was therefore no need for anything but the most simple accommodation aboard or the provision of even sitting head-room below decks. The long narrow cockpit was surrounded by low coamings, allowing wide side-decks, protected by a light six inch rail, for working the trawl. Aft the floor of the cockpit rose a foot to provide a platform for the helmsman. Amidships was a substantial thwart to give transversal strength to the hull. Beneath the floor and within reach of the helmsman, for the smaller shrimpers sometimes worked single-handed, was a hatch which gave access to a store where the anchor and cable were stowed. Iron ballast was beneath the cockpit floor amidships. Just aft of the mast a bulkhead, with a sliding door that opened into a cabin with a stove and lockers.

On deck there was no windlass, only a sampson post for belaying the cable on the fore-deck and aft, on either quarter two strong posts, known as 'knogs'. These were for directing the trawl rope. When trawling, the warp was always made secure forward of the mast to one of two timberheads and in the event of the trawl becoming caught on the seabed the helmsman could disengage the rope from the 'knog' close by him and the shrimper would come head to tide. No mechanical assistance was employed to bring home the trawl before the days when motors were fitted to the prawners. The ground rope of the trawl was threaded with bobbins of wood which made its progress over the bottom of Morecambe Bay easier. On some of the prawners a boiler was fitted and the catch was prepared for sale on board.

The Isle of Man Nobby

The Isle of Man herring fishery was an important basic industry of the Manx economy. It had long been carried out by open boats which had an obvious Scandinavian ancestry. These were originally square-rigged but a cutter sail-plan had been adopted in the late eighteenth century. They were fine seaworthy boats but the appearance of the Cornish fishing-luggers finding their way into the Irish Sea in the eighteen sixties, made the Manxmen realise that the decked luggers of the Duchy were a superior vessel. The fishing grounds were some thirty to forty miles from Port St. Mary and the power and speed of the Cornish luggers which brought the catch to port in prime condition excited the admiration of the local fishermen.

The St. Ives boat-builder William Paynter opened a yard at Kilkeel in Ireland and was soon producing craft to the Cornish pattern. Very soon Manx builders were also constructing to the Cornish model, luggers which were known as 'Nickeys'. This is said to derive from the frequency with which the name Nicholas was found amongst the men of the visiting fishing fleet. A few were built with counter-sterns to give an increased deckspace and the Manx boats usually tended to be somewhat larger than the Cornish craft.

In the eighteen eighties a change was made in the rig by substituting a standing lugsail on the foremast and setting a narrow foresail on the forestay. These luggers were known as

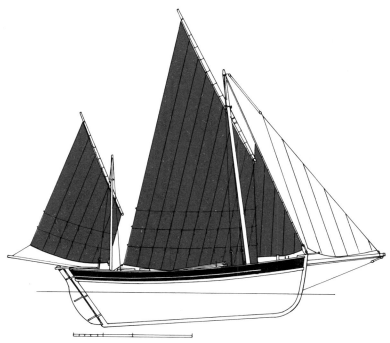

'nobbies'; they required a less skilled crew when going about than the older boats, but nevertheless it was conceded that they were not so speedy as their predecessors. The nobbies also had a bowsprit for setting the appropriate headsail for the weather; three sails of diminishing size were carried in the locker. Unlike the Cornishmen they did not change sails when reducing canvas: they fitted the sails with reef-points and three rows were provided on both the foresail and mizzen. The nobbies tended to be rather smaller than their companions, about 30 to 35 ft. on the keel.

Besides fishing in the immediate vicinity of the Isle of Man the nobbies ventured as far afield as the Shetlands, even traversing the Pentland Firth and fishing on the East Coast, while the west coast of Ireland was commonly reached. In October the herring could be caught in Douglas Bay and during the summer off the Calf of Man, but for the rest of the year the Manx fishermen were far from home landing their catches where they could. Mackerel were also caught but it was a fish which had to be sold the day it was netted and scorned the application of salt or ice to revive its fading glory. A binnacle, fitted into the sky-light companion, just forward of the mizzen-mast was an essential piece of equipment for this voyaging.

Hand capstans, for hauling in the warp, were fitted prior to 1881 and the crew numbered seven men and a boy. These capstans were turned by two handles on opposite sides of the vertical barrel. In 1881 steam capstans came into general use and it enabled the crews to be reduced to six men. The 'nickeys' and the larger nobbies carried a small boat on deck for getting ashore in remote places; when voyaging far afield fresh water had often to be obtained from a burn.

Today the fishing ports on the Isle of Man are no longer witnesses to the great fleets of luggers of the days of sail and the twentieth century has seen a rapid decline; the number of Manx-owned boats is one tenth of its former strength and the smoke-houses stand empty and neglected.

The Welsh Topsail Schooner

The rig of the small commercial sailing ship in the last quarter of the nineteenth century and the beginning of our own, was that of a topsail schooner. While schooners were owned all round the British coast it is convenient for the purposes of this book to associate them with the Western coast, for here they were launched in the greatest numbers and Portmadoc on Cardigan Bay, now a forgotten harbour, had a large fleet. In their later years the schooners were forced to seek their cargoes in the home-trade, cargoes of china clay and coal, and it is in this trade they are probably best remembered. But many of them were originally intended for much more adventurous voyaging. Schooners from Portmadoc of less than 90 ft. overall sailed to Hamburg with slates, they loaded fruit in Greece and salt in Spain; they sailed across the Atlantic to fetch cargoes of salt-cod from Newfoundland and hides from South America.

The rig had begun to appear in the western ports in the 1830's and from then on, because it was handier and more economical in canvas and cordage, it replaced the much older brig. Slightly larger vessels, rigged with three masts appeared in the 1870's. It was in the fruit trade to the Mediterranean that the schooner rig first showed its advantages, and beautifully equipped topsail schooners raced back from the Azores and the Mediterranean with valuable cargoes of fresh fruit ripening in their holds. When steamers captured this trade the schooners had to find alternative employment. These were the cream of the

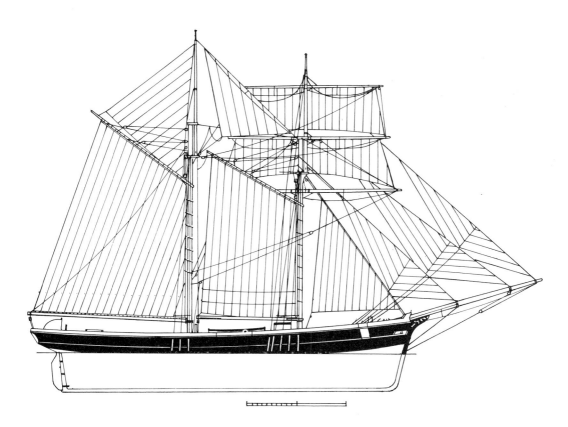

schooner fleet, others were more utilitarian in rig and build. They were built with a full
bilge so that they could conveniently lie upright in drying harbours and load the maximum
cargo. Topgallant yards became a rarity although they still set a large square-sail under
the foreyard when the wind was on the quarter and even a stunsail complete with boom,
hoisted to the upper yardarm and secured to the rail.

At first all schooners had long tillers, but later a wheel for steering and a wheelhouse
became usual. Forward of the wheelhouse was a skylight, which held the binnacle and
then came a substantial companion-way, often of teak. This led to the cabin for the master
and mate and also the mess cabin where the crew all ate together. The crew lived forward
in the forecastle, above which was the hard-worked windlass. Three hatches gave access
to the hold. One small one was foreward of the foremast, another, much larger, aft of it
and upon which the schooner's boat was lashed down when at sea; a third hatch was
placed aft of the main mast. Cooking was done in a diminutive wooden galley on deck,
fixed in position by iron straps. Close by one of the masts was a heavy wooden dolly
winch, sometimes in later times replaced by an iron one. This was for assistance when
setting sail, but particularly for working out the cargo, for it was part of the crew's duty to
undertake this laborious work. The crew of a schooner in the twentieth century was rarely
more than four or five – the advantage of the fore and aft rig lay largely in its capability of
being handled by a small crew. Roller reefing was commonly fitted on one or more of the
main fore and aft sails and this made reducing sail much easier.

Three topsail schooners were still trading coastwise at the outbreak of the Second
World War and a much larger number were working as auxiliaries, still setting a fair
spread of canvas. Now even these have gone or have become purely motor vessels.

The Swansea Pilot Schooner

Unlike nearly every other group of pilots, those of Swansea favoured the schooner-rig for their boats. It perpetuated a style of rigging small craft that was popular in the eighteenth century; known as shallops, they are frequently to be found represented in paintings of roadsteads and harbours on both sides of the Atlantic. The old harbour of Swansea dried out almost completely and faced into the prevailing south-west winds; it was common in the late eighteenth and early nineteenth century for the haven at the mouth of the Tawe to become packed with wind-bound shipping. At such times it was important for the local pilots to be able to get out to sea and assist the ships running to the port for safety. They needed weatherly craft which could come alongside a rolling square-rigger without the danger of fouling its yards and ropework. When putting a pilot aboard it was essential that the sails of the boat could be lowered in a moment and then hoisted quickly again upon sheering off from the side of the ship, a miniature schooner-rig met these requirements.

The early boats, although clinker-built and only 21 ft. long, were all schooner-rigged. Later they gradually grew in size but their growth was limited by the fact that sometimes they had to return to port and dock single-handed. The crew usually consisted of a master, two paid hands, and three pilots on the outward passage. By the mid-nineteenth century carvel construction had become usual and boats were built with full bows and a square wide transom stern, about 30 ft. overall. The unusually short gaffs were deliberately fitted

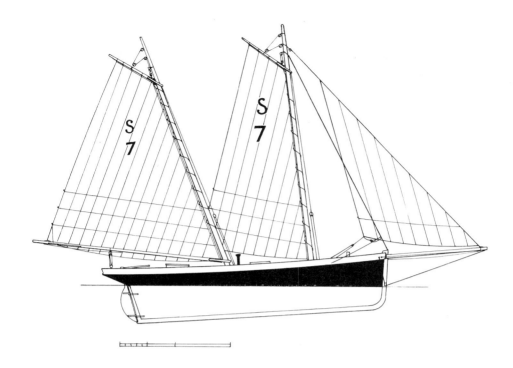

to facilitate their handling in a sea-way. They also made it possible for the throat halliards on both gaffs to be dispensed with, thus leaving only the single peak halliard. On the foremast the halliard at the peak of the gaff in latter-day boats was occasionally rove through a block at the throat so that the single rope served for both throat and peak halliard. There were no shrouds, but the halliards could be led to the weather gunwale and secured to support the mast if the boat was being pressed hard in a breeze. A sliding bowsprit with a single jib, set flying, was carried.

The enlargement of Swansea Dock in 1859 increased the volume of foreign tonnage coming to the port. The pilots now ranged further out, seeking homeward bounders, occasionally as far afield as Lands End and Milford. When in harbour the boats could now berth in the tidal basin of the dock, so that they were no longer dried out on the ebb tide; this enabled a sharper, steeper floored hull-form to be adopted with a draught of six to eight feet. But the Swansea men still remained faithful to the schooner-rig. One of its advantages was that when running in heavy weather it was convenient for the foresail, made up from heavier canvas, to be used alone; when in port the main boom, like the bowsprit, was unshipped and run in, to avoid damage.

The contracting of Swansea's foreign trade in the eighteen nineties, together with changes in the pilotage regulations brought the beginning of the end to the days of the schooners. They no longer had the necessity to 'go seeking' far from their home port down the Bristol Channel. Now, with shortened main booms, they towed a 10 ft. punt for putting pilots aboard steamers approaching the port. Finally, in 1898, the steam pilot cutter arrived and six years later the surviving two schooners, the *Grenfell* (S.9) and the *Benson* (S.4), hitherto retained in a standby capacity, were sold.

The Tenby Lugger

Tenby on the western end of the Carmarthen Bay possesses a harbour which was once packed with fishing craft and small trading vessels. Trawlers from Brixham, oyster skiffs from the Mumbles as well as the locally owned craft were to be found there. Besides the larger decked vessels, many of which were built at Brixham for Tenby owners, there were numerous open boats. These craft were substantially built luggers and unlike the vast majority of West Country craft did not show the influence of Cornish builders. They were full-bowed and had a comfortable eighteenth century feeling about their lines. Clench built and deep-keeled, with a full midship section, they were on average 22 ft. overall but tended to be built larger as older boats were replaced.

The fore part of the Tenby lugger was decked to the mainmast and beneath the decking was a small cuddy with access provided by a sliding hatch in the bulkhead. There were usually three rowing thwarts and a thwart and quarter benches in the stern for the helmsman. Ballast was carried in the bilge beneath a substantial floor, supported by beams. The luggers had the advantage of lying to moorings and were not hauled out except for servicing, so that they could be built with a heavy keel, some 18 ins. deep. Heavy oak floor timbers were fitted and alternated with bent frames. The mainmast was stepped about one-third of the boat's length from the stempost. To starboard of the rudderhead the mizzen was stepped on the transom and followed its rake. A bowsprit was

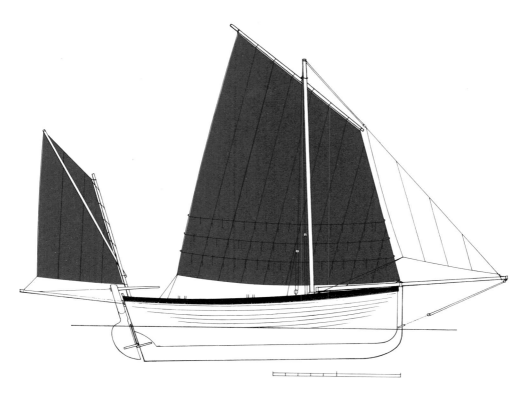

carried through a gammon iron on the stemhead and the outrigger for the mizzen sheet was stepped through a hole in the transom. The mainsail was a dipping lug, with two or three rows of reef points and was replaced in winter by a trysail, held to the mast with hoops and only carried when working the oyster beds. Three jibs of various sizes were set appropriate to the strength of the wind; a small spritsail was set on the mizzen.

The luggers were maids-of-all-work; they were used for line and drift-net fishing, for oyster-dredging and putting unofficial pilots aboard visiting trading vessels. Line fishing, both with hand lines and long-lines, was their traditional occupation, but the big ketch-rigged trawlers were often sweeping the same area that the luggers used, with the inevitable result that the luggers' lines were carried away. Eventually the luggers were forced to work only those grounds where the rough bottom discouraged the trawlers. Some drift-net fishing for herring was done but Carmarthen Bay never attracted the size of shoals found elsewhere. As compensation the Bay held a rarer resource in the form of oyster beds which lay north of Caldy Island. Other beds were a little south of Stackpole Head, although their distance from Tenby Harbour meant that the undecked luggers could only visit them for dredging in moderate weather. But inevitably with over exploitation and no cultivation or the transference of immature fish to 'nursery' beds, the area was gradually worked out. Besides the Tenby boats, oyster skiffs came from the Mumbles area, where there were also beds, and they worked the area in addition to the smaller local trawlers. By the end of the nineteenth century only enough oysters were dredged to satisfy a purely local market. The luggers and their crews were finding an alternative employment and one much less arduous than heaving and hauling iron dredges off Caldy Isle, in providing trips for summer visitors. With the development of Milford Haven, provided by nature with a magnificent natural harbour, Tenby ceased to be used and today its landings of fish are negligible.

The Galway Hooker

The rock-bound coast of Connermara, in the far west of Ireland, faces the grey Atlantic seas and is a remote land of rock and mountain. The people who live there have always looked to the sea for part of their hard-won livelihood. Their traditional craft and one that has been in use over the centuries for fishing is the curragh, a primitive survival from a prehistoric past. The curraghs, some of which are up to 17 ft. in length, are built from a simple wickerwork frame of ash fitted to heavy wooden gunwales, which are connected aft by a similar athwartship timber. The framework is then covered over with tarred canvas.

Although the fragile curragh may be pressed into service to carry peat or to ferry livestock, it is essentially a fishing boat. For cargo-carrying the hooker was used, until made redundant by the adoption of the twentieth century ways of life, within the last decade. It was the last native sailing craft in commercial use in Ireland and preserved the small trading smack rig. The hooker was a fine, able sailing craft, built in Connemara or Galway, a gaff cutter of 35 ft. to 40 ft. overall and used until recently to load peat, more general cargoes, and occasionally passengers.

A hooker was built of larch planking on heavy sawn frames of oak; when fully loaded it carried about eight tons of cargo and was handled by two men. She was decked forward of the mast only and had a very pronounced sheer; to protect the hold wash strakes were fitted and reached to the mast. The hull had an unusually marked tumble-home, probably

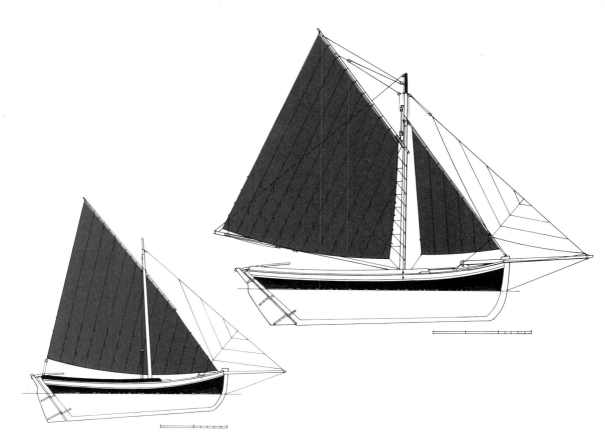

to make it more convenient for the vessel to lie against the walls of the West Irish harbours, which all dry out. The transom stern raked strongly aft and was combined with a sharply rising floor and a long keel for the hookers were adapted to a deep water coast where they could either keep afloat or lie alongside a harbour wall. The hookers, unchanged in general design for well over a century, were rigged in the simplest possible manner with a heavy, short mast supported by a single shroud on either side, and characteristically bowed forward to give a better set to the luff of the mainsail. The mainsail was high peaked and only loosely laced to the mast. The hookers were occasion-ally used for long line fishing, although their name derives, not from this occupation, but from the ancient word 'urca', of foreign origin and meaning a small fore and aft rigged craft, which the Irish in time corrupted to 'hooker'. The ocean off the West Irish coast teams with fish but the remote nature of the area, cut off from any sizeable market left it undeveloped and likewise the little hooker remained a vessel from the past.

Smaller vessels, of a similar basic type, employed in the same area, were the gleotogs; they were about 28 to 30 ft. overall and, like the hookers were turf-carriers and sometimes served for passenger-carrying and fishing. The smaller 'poucan' was of a similar form, sharing the same type of a raking transom stern and pronounced tumble-home of the larger craft, only quite open and rigged with a high peaked dipping lug, augmented by a jib set on a running bowsprit. The 'poucan' was essentially a fishing boat, although occasion-ally pressed into service to carry cargoes of kelp.

Within the last twenty years the little craft, setting their deeply tanned sails, could be seen in nearly every bay from Cashla to Creggan. Now a few survive converted to yachts, as auxiliaries and as fishing craft for the tourists.

The Severn Trow

If the trow had few pretentions to nautical grace, she could lay claim to a name that indicated an origin in medieval times. Trow is an ancient word closely linked with trough and the bluff bows, open hold and square stern of the trow makes the connection clear. They began as the river trading vessel of the Severn and its tributaries, reaching far inland and carrying industrial products from Ironbridge and coal from the old pits of the Forest of Dean. In those days their rig was a single square-sail, although it seems that the trows that ventured into the estuary had a mizzen and bowsprit. When the railways took much of the inland trade hitherto moved by water, the trows were employed to carry cargoes in the Severn Estuary and to the newly developed Welsh coal-ports. Sloop rigged trows known as 'witch barges' brough salt down from Droitwich to Gloucester for transhipment into schooners until the nineteen hundreds.

A sloop rig and then that of a ketch replaced the squaresail, with a long bowsprit set beside the stemhead, although a few with squaresails were working until the eighteen seventies. Many trows were lengthened amidships but still retained the traditional open hold, protected by side-cloths, held up by stanchions and reinforced with wooden boards. Although trows reached as far as Milford Haven and the Cornish coast, generally speaking and not unnaturally, trading with such vulnerable craft was limited to a line

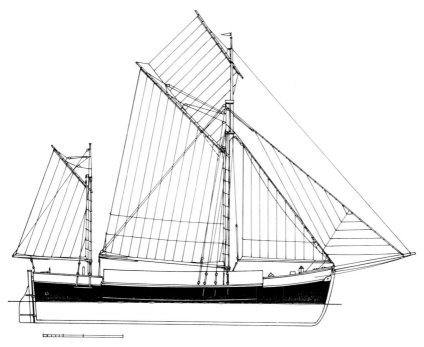

drawn between Watchet on the Somerset side of the Severn Sea and Barry on the Welsh shore. Some trow-owners fitted their vessels with bulwarks and side decks and these were known as 'box trows'; others were given bulwarks and hatch coamings at the ends of the hold but they retained the open hold amidships; these were called 'half box trows'. A number of sloop-rigged iron trows were built.

A typical trow would be difficult to find for there were many varieties, but one that survived into the twentieth century would be 70 ft. overall, with a broad, deep transom stern and a beam of 17 ft. and draw some 6 ft. loading about 70 tons. They were all flat bottomed and some were actually constructed with floors which sloped slightly upwards towards the keel so that they could take the ground safely. In order to improve their limited sailing ability some trows had a removable keel, two feet deep, which was manoeuvred into position and held by chains. The trows after the eighteen seventies were expressedly launched for estuary work and a number were built at Bridgwater and their form was nearer that of a conventional ketch. They had a normal but rather shallow external keel and massive keelson, flat floors and their decking was restricted to a short length at the bow and stern, beneath which was the master's accommodation. Carrying bunkering coal to steamers was a regular trade for many trows and their wooden cros-strees were constructed to fold upwards to prevent any damage to the rigging when coming alongside. The two-man crew of a trow were worked hard. They had to manage the old-fashioned rig and a long line was carried on the top barrel of the dolly winch for warping in docks and along riverside quays. Forward in the bows was an old-fashioned hand-spike windlass; few had the relatively modern pump-handle type. Their heavily built boat was always astern in readiness for towing in order to negotiate awkward reaches of the rivers which they traded.

The trows were extraordinarily long lived. The best known centenarian amongst them was the *William* of Gloucester, built in 1809 as a square-rigged trow, later converted to ketch-rig and lost, still at work, in 1939. Another, the *Palace,* was working for nearly as long and had been built in 1827. The last survived as unrigged lighters on the Bristol Avon.

The Bristol Channel Pilot Cutter

Last of the pilots to relinquish cruising under sail were those of the Bristol Channel. Their cutters were the best known of all the pilot craft and rightly so; they were immensely varied, but all were fine, powerful sea-keeping craft. A fleet of no less than one hundred cutters, or 'skiffs' as they were known locally, were serving shipping in the Bristol Channel in the years immediately preceding the First World War. At that time a huge tonnage of shipping was trading to the Welsh coal-ports, besides Bristol and later Avonmouth. The pilots cruised a wide territory seeking ships to board, which covered not only the Severn Sea but the English Channel and Irish Sea as well.

There was great competition amongst the pilots to own or use the fastest, weatherly and most sea-kindly boat with the result that there was a very wide difference of hull-form amongst the skiffs. Size was limited by the fact that after the pilots had boarded ships, two men or only a man and a boy apprentice, would remain aboard to bring the craft home to port. The smallest skiff was little more than 30 ft. while the largest was nearly 60 ft. overall. There was a tendency for the pilots to order larger boats as each new skiff was launched and from averaging 40 ft. in the 1870s they eventually, in the nineteen hundreds, measured 50 ft. from bow to stern. The oldest were square-sterned, but elliptical counters

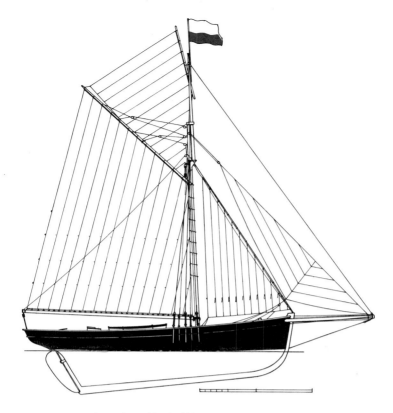

and transom sterns were introduced by builders and the only common denominator of the skiffs was a high bow and freeboard. Many cutters were built at Pill on the Avon, but pilots ordered boats from Fleetwood, Penarth and Cornish builders seeking a better skiff to compete with their colleagues. The traditional underwater lines were a long straight keel and rounded forefoot with ballast carried inside amidships. Later craft had some ballast in the keel and many were fitted with watertight cockpits for the helmsman. The qualities that were sought above all in a skiff were the ability to heave-to and ride the seas with an easy motion, making life tolerable for those on board.

By day the cutters flew a red and white pilot flag at the topmast-head: at night a blue flare was burnt every 15 minutes. The pilots boarded the ships directly in fine weather; if the seas did not permit this they worked their cutter under the leeside and one of the hands took the pilot across in the skiff's 'punt' – a heavily built boat 13 ft. long. If the cutter was short-handed the pilot rowed himself to the foot of the ship's boarding ladder and then kicked away the punt which was picked up by the skiff. It was usual for only one man to be on deck to sail the skiffs and so the sail-plan was necessarily simple. Only relatively short topmasts were carried, setting a variety of topsails, they were usually set to starboard and remained there. The skiffs were well known for their early acceptance of roller-reefing. This was fitted to the inboard end of the main-boom and was worked by rotating a worm-gear by a handle which rolled the sail around the boom. It replaced the tedious process of using reef tackles and reef points, but was hard on the sail and brought an undue strain on the boom. In winter, a smaller, heavy-duty flax mainsail was carried to be replaced by a lighter cotton canvas one in summer.

The *Cariad*, built in 1904 by E. Rowles of Pill near Bristol, after long service as pilot skiff and a cruising yacht, is now preserved at Exeter Maritime Museum.

The Falmouth Quay Punt

In the days of deep-water sail Falmouth, with its fine expanse of protected water was a convenient port of arrival and anchorage for ships. In the roadstead lay square-riggers awaiting orders for the ultimate destination of their cargo – their crews effecting repairs or looking for a fair wind to take them up Channel. The quay punts were owned by local boatmen who tended the vessels in the anchorage; they put captains ashore, ferried out fresh food, delivered stores and took chandlers and agents aboard. As the punts lay at deep-water moorings when not in use, they could be built with a deep keel, while on the other hand their work took them alongside square-rigged ships and so they were modestly masted in order that their gear did not foul the yardarms and rigging.

The early punts were clench-built lug-rigged open boats of about 18 ft. with the foremast stepped well up in the bows and, like the Cornish fishing boats, the mizzen sail sheeted to a long outrigger. Punts of this type co-existed for working close inshore long after the improved carvel-planked version was developed by the boatmen. The newer boats began to appear in the 1870s when, with the coming of steam, a brisker and more competitive tempo developed. To seek potential customers the punts had to go further to the westward and for working to seaward a craft some 30 ft. overall developed. They were decked for two-thirds of their length and had waterways on either side of the well and a short deck in the stern. The hulls had a typically Cornish form, with the greatest beam aft of amidships and a narrow, sharp bow. Although the boats of the eighteen eighties had

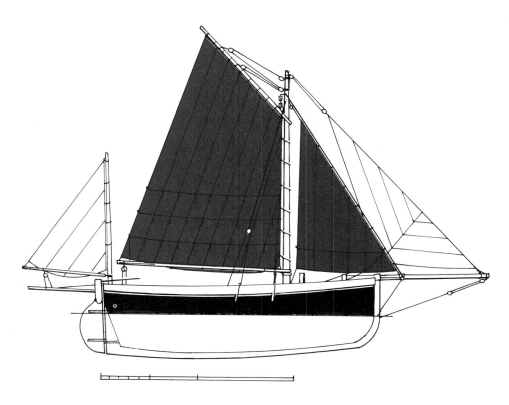

long, straight keels and a vertical stem and stern, the punts built at the turn of the century modified this design, when the days of sail were drawing to a close and the tradition of 'hovelling' was almost over. A raked stern-post and rockered keel, with outside ballast influenced by yacht design, was introduced. All types had common factors in a transom stern and yawl rig. Besides their ordinary duties punts took out pleasure parties and were used for mackerel fishing in summer.

The yawl rig was appropriate for it enabled a punt to jog along at sea under mizzen and foresail, awaiting a homeward bounder off the Lizard. The punts would leave their moorings off Custom House Quay at Falmouth in the small hours, without navigation lights, to escape the notice of their competitors and would work to the westward seeking a ship. When they had secured an acknowledgment from a ship bound for Falmouth and their services were required, the punt would accompany her into the anchorage and tend her as long as she was in the port.

The punt's rig was simple; an iron bumkin on the bow extended the foresail's tack and a bowsprit and jib were only carried in the summer. The tiller had a deep crank in it for working round the mizzen; this was stepped to port to give it as much play as possible. A leg-of-mutton mizzen sail was set normally, but a large standing lug was substituted in fine weather and when racing in regattas where they were always well represented and competition was keen. Quay punts were perhaps the first work-boats to have their potential qualities exploited by yacht-designers seeking small cruising boats. Many punts were purchased and converted for this purpose. Long after the original usefulness of their design had passed away, cruising yachtsmen ordered craft to be built on the quay punt's lines.

The Polperro Gaffer

Despite continual battering by the sea, which has threatened its very existence, the little Cornish fishing village of Polperro has long maintained a fishing fleet sheltered in its natural harbour. The boats were engaged in line-fishing and principally caught whiting, ling and then cod. Netting pilchard in August brought the best rewards from the sea, which at best were modest, but this lasted only until October when the shoals moved on. In 1891 a severe gale swept heavy seas into the harbour and caused havoc amongst the fleet seeking refuge. These were large open boats, clinker-built and sprit-rigged, with a topsail and a lug mizzen. They were replaced after the gale by gaff-rigged carvel-built boats built by two builders at Looe, a few miles down the coast, J. Pearce and Oliver. The new boats were gaff-rigged without a boom for this would have restricted movement when fishing. They had a small cuddy in the bows and the mast was stepped in the keelson and supported by a substantial beam a few feet aft of the cuddy bulkhead. They were referred to as 'gaffers' to distinguish them from their ill-fated predecessors that carried a spritsail. The deck was little more than a narrow waterway rather more than a foot below the level of the gunwale; amidships a bulkhead divided the net room from the fish hold. Another

bulkhead separated this from a raised platform for the helmsman; through this platform an iron pump projected for clearing the bilge. A wooden roller spanned the full width of the hull, over the fish room; this was used for scudding the nets as they were hauled in.

The gaffers were about 25 ft. overall and had a 9 ft. beam, the widest point being slightly aft of amidships. They had a steep midship section and had to be fitted with legs, bolted to a stanchion, to remain upright when they dried out; many had deepwater moorings in the harbour. The wide transom stern raked aft slightly and they drew about 6 ft. aft. The fishermen aimed to keep the mast as short as possible, for, unlike the luggers, they could not lower them when fishing as they lay to their nets or lines. In a swell a tall mast had a pendulum effect and increased any tendency to roll. The mainsail was augmented by a large yard topsail which the Polperro men set with great style by reeving the tack through a block on the gaff, shackled on just short of the gaff jaws. They even contrived to send aloft a jib topsail by setting up the tack-rope of the sail through a block on the bowsprit end, itself a very long spar. The halliard passed through a block at the head of the topsail yard. The mainsheet was rove through two double blocks, one hooked to the sail and the other working across an iron horse in the transom. This unconventional sail-plan and the niceties of setting it to the best advantage were a source of pride to the Polperro crews and were recognised at the time. When the wind failed a long sweep was used and a sculling notch in the transom was cut to accommodate it. As the long-lines were hauled in the boy member of the crew stood by with a 'kieve net' to retrieve any fish that escaped from the hooks as they came aboard. Motors were fitted to the boats during the First World War and for a time fishing continued from Polperro, but on a diminishing scale. Now Polperro looks to the tourist rather than the sea to gain a livelihood.

The East Cornish Lugger

Just as the shoals of herring brought work to the many and wealth to a few along the East Coast, so the pilchard and mackerel dominated the lives of the Cornish fishermen. On the west coast of the Duchy, between Gwennap Head and the Lizard, with Penzance as its centre, man-made harbours hold precariously to a rugged shore-line. These are supplemented by a few restricted natural coves which, like the harbours, dry out at low-water. South-easterly winds and spring tides bring with them a heavy swell which makes even these modest havens uncomfortable for small ships. When the luggers sought safety they were forced to nose their way in amongst a welter of craft; to facilitate this, east Cornish fishing boats were built with sharp sterns. This minimised the likelihood of damage at close quarters, whilst a massive rubbing strake along the hull gave an added protection when the luggers were crammed together. The west Cornish craft were better served, for they had better natural harbours which provided more elbow room; the boat builders of St. Ives could therefore construct their luggers with square transom sterns which gave the advantage of a wider working area on deck. Carvel construction provided an added strength to the hulls which were severely tested as the luggers were pounded on the harbour floor when the tide made and ebbed.

Their lugsail rig reflected the requirements of drift-net fishing. Once the nets were shot, the main-mast was lowered to a few feet above the deck and a small mizzen sail was set to keep the vessel riding the Atlantic rollers, head to wind. Unlike the East Coasters, who

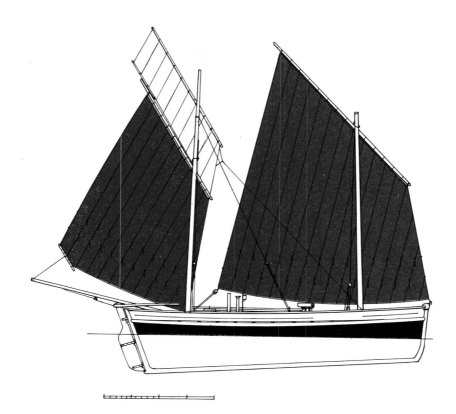

also drifted for demersial fish and who had adopted the gaff rig, the Cornish men, working over the wide, deep waters off their native shores, did not require the same capacity for working smartly to windward with shorter tacks. The working sails of a Cornish boat were so cut that those set as standing lugs on the mizzen might be hoisted as dipping lugs on the main-mast. The characteristic upward rake of the outrigger noticeable on the drawing, set to port of the rudder head over the stern, facilitated this. As the wind freshened, the main sail was lowered and stowed in the iron crutches on the port rail; the mizzen took its place and a smaller after sail was substituted. This process was repeated as necessary and the storm-weather mizzen, known as the jigger, was hoisted; finally, as a last resort, a spare jigger was always carried so that in extreme conditions this could be set, reefed, on the mainmast.

The fishing luggers of the Duchy ranged far and wide. They worked off the Lizard for mackerel, the Irish Sea for herring, and then, by means of the Caledonian Canal, reached the North Sea, some venturing as far as the Shetland Isles. The season was concluded in early October, by which time they were landing their catches at Scarborough and Whitby. The long passage home provided an opportunity for the luggers to show their prowess; a light bowsprit was lashed to the stern-head and a jib set when the wind was aft of the beam, while a mizzen staysail might be hoisted between the masts. It was common for some of the ballast below decks to be piled up to windward when sailing hard out to the fishing grounds. When homeward bound, this was augmented by heaving the jolly-boat, carried on deck, to windward and filling it with water. On one memorable occasion in 1910 three luggers made passage from Mount's Bay to Scarborough, a distance of nearly 600 miles, in only 70 hours.

The Brixham Trawler

The Brixham trawling fleet ten years before the First World War was one of the finest array of powerful sailing fishing vessels to be seen on any European coast. Its origins went deep into Devon history. Brixham was at a disadvantage for the working of seine nets which was the traditional Devon fishery, for it had few adjacent open beaches. But its harbour was convenient for boats to work the fishing grounds of the two great bays where the quality ground fish were to be caught.

It is said that the Brixham men were the first to develop the fish-trawl; it seems certain that the combination of effective gear, speedy ships and a reasonably handy market at Exeter and Bath, where a luxury trade existed, resulted in the formation of a fishing fleet at about 1770. Much of the best ground for fishing was in the lee of the Skerries, running northward from Start Point. It was particularly suitable for the sailing trawlers, which needed a really fresh breeze to work in successfully, without too heavy a swell to strain their tackle.

The ketch rig replaced the older cutter rig as the bigger boats were introduced in the seventies and the older cutters were lengthened. It was a change stimulated by the railway which had reached and spread throughout the South West peninsular. With bigger smacks the handspike of the horizontal windlass was replaced by the capstan which in turn was followed by the steam driven winch. These innovations made it possible to carry a longer beam trawl and handle it with greater safety. The more powerful boats could make

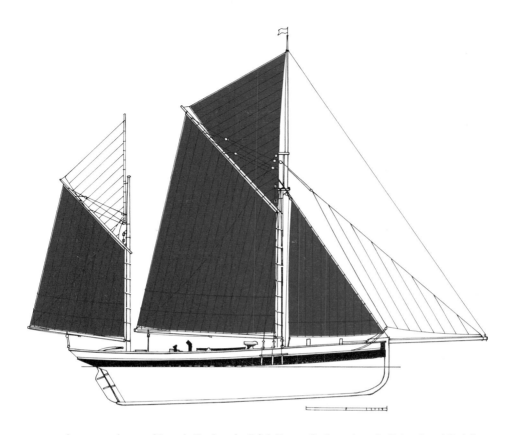

seasonal voyages beyond Lands End to the Irish Sea to find markets in Bristol and Dublin. Enterprising Devon men had been working from Ramsgate since the mid-century, then venturing to Scarborough and Grimsby, at first to fish and then to settle. The ketches were magnificent craft. The largest were 77 ft. overall, with an 18 ft. 6 in. beam, drawing 11 ft. aft and built with a fine sweeping sheer. The sternpost was raked and while most of the trawlers were built with a square counter, latterly an elliptical one became popular. The masts had a forward rake and although not lofty, the sail plan could be augmented by a big 'tow foresail' when trawling, and topsails, with yards, were set on both masts in summer calms. It was common practice to carry a jib-headed topsail over a reefed mainsail in a breeze, Brixham craft used reef lacings instead of reefing points to save wear on sails. A seaman crouched in the belly of the sail as the smack lay hove-to and threaded the lacing through the eyes while his mates stood-by to draw it tight.

Limited quay space, meagre rail facilities were all adverse factors to be set against risking large investment of capital involved with the introduction of steam trawlers at Brixham. When war broke out in 1914 many fishermen who were Naval Reservists were called up and vessels were laid up, and although they returned it was to a very different world. There were numerous sunken ships along the coast which made 'fasts' for the nets, and the North Sea fishery was, after lying fallow, providing a prodigious bounty which forced down prices. A few sailing ketches were launched, one of the last the *Forseti* in 1926, but more were laid up or converted to cruising yachts. There were still 29 ketches working under sail from Brixham in 1936. The *Provident,* converted to a yacht, is now owned by the Maritime Trust and is to be restored to her former appearance as a fishing ketch.

The Beer Lugger

The Beer luggers were South Devon beach-boats, launching and landing on a shore ringed with red cliffs which, from the fisherman's point of view, had just enough shelter to protect it from gales and sea-swell and to enable a longshoreman to earn a precarious livelihood. They were open except for a 'cutty' forward and were rigged with fore, main and mizzen lugsails. Although the main mast had long since been abandoned elsewhere on the coast, the three-masted rig had survived at Beer until the First World War. The Beer boats were also unusual in that they fitted a long iron bumkin on the stemhead. This raked sharply downward and was fitted with two hooks which provided alternative positions for the tack of the mainsail, reefed and unreefed. This method, by which the tack of the foresail is brought down to almost sea-level is nearly unique. Another interesting survival used aboard the Beer luggers was a spar, or 'foreguard' as it was locally called, to thrust forward the luff of the foresail when sailing hard on the wind and prevent it shaking. When in use the spar was fitted into a cringle on the luff of the sail while the butt was lashed to the foot of the foremast by a rope permanently rove through a hole in the spar. While the 'foreguard' enabled the foresail to set well going to windward a bowline led from the luff of the mainsail to the foremast and was hauled taut. Going about with such an arrangement must have been a well rehearsed drill to avoid trouble. Shingle in sacks was carried as ballast and thrown into the weather bilge on a long tack.

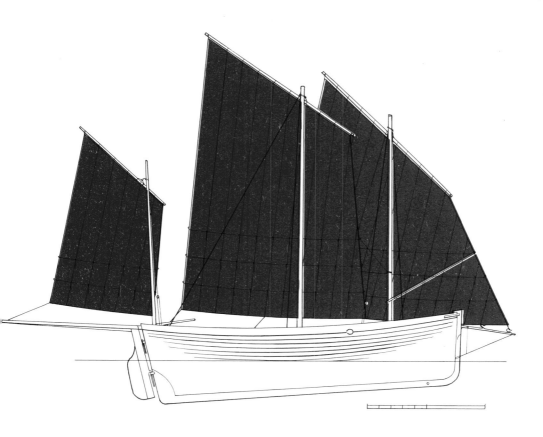

Beer luggers were clench-built with rather flat floors and a transom stern; they were bought from builders at Exmouth for Beer had no local builder. The three-masters were some 28 ft. overall, 11 ft. 6 ins. beam and were 5 ft. deep and fitted with four thwarts. One of their more important catches was mackerel, caught with hand-lines, which were towed at such a speed as to encourage the fish to bite, and for this reason the Beer fishermen retained their powerful three-masted rig so long. The big luggers rigged out poles on either beam to work six lines simultaneously when mackerel fishing; luggers never tacked but wore round so as to avoid getting the lines foul under the keel. Fishing in an open boat was a harsh business; an old fish box half-filled with pebbles upon which was burnt a piece of tow soaked in paraffin served as a stove to boil a kettle. The crew snatched such sleep as they might on the lowered sails or in the 'cutty' in the bows. Drifting for herring was another major occupation, involving 240 fathoms of net. Ironically a successful haul could all too easily load a boat down until she was unseaworthy. When it reached the landing loaded down in this way, some of her nets and catch would, if possible, be ferried ashore before beaching was attempted.

The South Devon beach boatmen had the good fortune to find an articulate friend in Stephen Reynolds who wrote about their life with rare insight and without sentimentality. He encouraged the installation of motors and after about 1915 the three-masters were replaced by rather smaller two-masted boats where the sails were auxiliary. The extra weight of the engine encouraged a shorter hull to be built and the last of the old craft was broken up in 1918.

The West Country Barge

The life and seamanship of the two-man crews of the West Country sailing barges may have been of an unheroic order but it must have been, compared with the existence of others who earned a living on the water, a relatively pleasant one. The barges traded about the estuaries of the Tamar and Fal, Plymouth Sound and the adjoining coast, taking cargoes far into the Cornish and Devon countryside. The barges were divided by build and rig into two classes. The 'inside barges' only rarely ventured outside the official limits of sheltered waters and could be loaded down until their freeboard was measured in inches. They were to be found working about the wooded inland creeks and little harbours until finally they could no longer compete with road transport. The larger 'outside barges' normally had a Board of Trade load line, were more heavily rigged and were capable of trading up Channel. They had to choose their time for they were not designed to withstand heavy weather at sea.

All the barges were gaff-rigged. 'Inside barges' rarely carried a topmast, although a bowsprit was usually fitted, while the 'outsiders' carried a full cutter-rig. The 'inside barges' had their mast stepped in a tabernacle, or mast saddle, so that it could be lowered to enable the barge to work above bridges. 'Outside barges' had their masts stepped on the keelson and had three shrouds and a running backstay as part of their normal rigging. In fact their sail and rigging plan perpetuated that of the trading smacks of the early

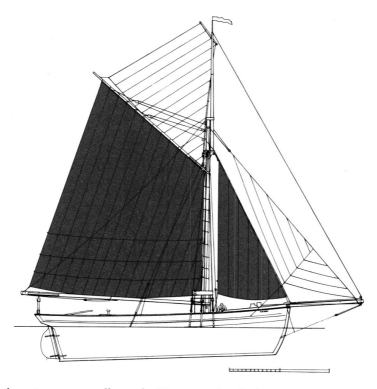

nineteenth century on a smaller scale. However, they had a very different hull form; they were much shallower – the draught of a big outside barge was never more than seven feet when fully loaded, although they were some 50 ft. overall, with a beam of 16 ft. Their lines, particularly the Cornish barges, had relatively sharp bows and a good run aft to a shallow transom or neat square counter stern – the latter a peculiarity of the Kingsbridge-built craft. The stem raked forward and the bow and forward rails flared outwards slightly – some indication of the untrammelled life they led. Such an arrangement would have had a short life in the brutal existence of an industrialised river. The sternpost raked aft and the forefoot was rounded; the floors were flat to give the hold the maximum capacity and to ensure that the barge remained upright when she dried out on a beach for landing a cargo.

The origin of the barges lies, on one hand, in a 'growing-up' of the open-hold market-boats of the Fal and the apple-bowed lightering barges, which, sloop-rigged and with an iron bumkin on the stemhead to set a foresail, worked on the Helford river. On the other hand the old heavier seagoing smacks provided the model for their rigging aloft and deck fittings. There were a few builders, like Goss of Calstock, who produced many barges, but they were launched in yards like Dyer's of Sunny Corner on the Tamar and F. Hawk's near Plymouth who were primarily builders of schooners.

The barges were all fitted with a handspike windlass in the bows and forward of the mast was an iron winch for handling the cargo and warping alongside quays. There was only one large hatch amidships and on this the 'outside barges' lashed down their boat when they went coasting, while the smaller barges always towed theirs astern. Fitting auxiliary engines began in the nineteen twenties, enabling barges to compete with less picturesque forms of transport, but now with no new vessels launched and the old ones inevitably becoming unseaworthy they have all passed away.

The West Country Trading Ketch

While the ketch-rigged trader was certainly not confined to the South West Peninsular, it survived longer there than elsewhere. The last traders under sail to its open beaches, its little stone harbours and the quays along its estuaries, were the ketches.

Many of the earlier ketches were smacks which were converted to the more easily handled ketch-rig by shortening the main boom and adding a mizzen mast, just beyond the arc made by the tiller end. In fact the ketch-rig was the final development of the wooden merchant sailing vessel in Britain. While some West Country ketches sailed quite regularly across the Atlantic, the majority were employed more prosaically in coasting, with occasional voyages to Continental ports. The rig was adopted on tiny vessels, barely 50 ft. long and on vessels built originally as 85-ft. schooners, loading 140 tons and then, as an economy measure, re-rigged as ketches. The ketch-rig became popular at first in the 1870s, not only for traders but for fishing boats as well. All the sails were of such a size as to be easily handled by a small crew. The point of sailing where a ketch was at a disadvantage was when running before the wind, for then an unintentional gybe could occur. Because of this many carried a squaresail which could be set from a yard temporarily sent aloft on the foresail halliard when the wind was astern. A small ketch would be worked with only two men and a boy (who was really an apprentice), or only master and mate. Handling ketches at sea was made easier after about nineteen hundred by the

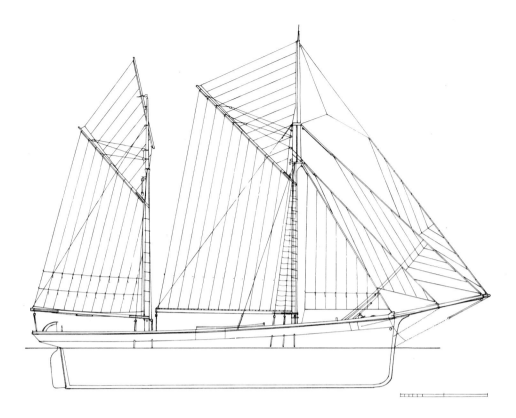

adoption of roller-reefing gear on the mainsail and sometimes the mizzen as well. Large gaff topsails were carried, usually set from the deck on a jackstay and fitted with a long yard at the head.

Few ketches carried a galley on deck; cooking was done in the fo'c'sle and the life was both hard and comfortless. The ketches carried bulk cargoes of coal, stone, slate, bricks and tiles. Salt was welcomed because it was said to help to preserve the wood hull. Bagged flour and food grains paid well while sand was a mere ballast freight that was only just worthwhile. While all the ketches could shift from one berth to another with an empty hold, to go to sea and sail effectively they required at least some ballast. Most of the cargoes had to be discharged by the crew working at the dolly winch and a spare gaff was always carried to be sent aloft with the throat and peak halliards to serve as a derrick. A removable section of the bulwarks amidships assisted loading and unloading and was convenient for launching the ketch's boat, normally lashed down on the main hatch. Ketches were small enough to land cargoes on beaches, some mere crevices in the rock, all round the South West Peninsular and on the Welsh Coast. While this earned more than the average freightage it was a hazardous business and if possible the discharging by farm carts was done in two tides to avoid experiencing an onshore wind with a ground swell which would drive the vessel up and down on the hard sand.

Auxiliary engines were fitted to a few West Country ketches immediately before the First World War and at its conclusion the numbers increased rapidly. When an engine was installed topmasts were sent down, triangular mizzens replaced the gaff sail and headsails reduced for, while the wind is free, sailmakers submit accounts. The last wooden auxiliary ketch did not cease commercial work until well after the Second World War.

137

The Itchen Ferry Boat

Although their name associates them with a Hampshire river it is something of a misnomer for these craft were found everywhere at 'the back of the Wight', not only on the Solent but on the Test and Hamble as well. Locally their work was within relatively sheltered waters so that they were only three-quarter decked, with a large cockpit aft and waterways running along either quarters terminating in a tiny trawl deck in the stern. They were relatively small and very beamy, between 16 and 30 ft. in length, and built with a transom stern and straight bow, well rounded at the foot so that it did not trap a warp when fishing. Their owners were much involved with yachting in the summer, acting as professional skippers or paid hands so that their boats had to be of such a size as could be easily laid up and then fitted out when the yachts went to their winter quarters.

Contact with the yachts developed a more than usually high competitive instinct amongst the fishermen. Their work boats did not have to take the ground at the moorings so that they could be built with deep draught. They had an extremely shapely hull with a reverse turn of the garboards and a keel shod with an iron shoe to give stability, although some internal ballast was carried. The hull was built, carvel fashion, of red pine planking, copper-fastened on oak frames; equally traditionally, all the wood work was thoroughly impregnated with linseed oil before painting.

The smacks rarely spent more than a day away and the smaller boats worked single-handed. It was just as well, for the tiny cuddy forward had barely 'sitting head-room', but was equipped with a stove and two berths. The craft rarely, if ever, carried topmasts and while the original boats were rigged with a narrow, boomless mainsail, they were all fitted with booms projecting well over the stern by the 'seventies and set yard topsails.

A boomless mainsail was still carried, fitted especially for the work when shrimping to give an opportunity for the crew to cull over a catch without danger of a gybe. The foresail tack was carried a foot or so beyond the stem by means of an iron bumkin, and the long bowsprit was shipped to starboard alongside it.

Besides trawling, both for shrimps and flatfish, dredging for oysters was part of their work, particularly at the end of the autumn. This was supplemented by stow-boat netting for sprats between October and February. As may well be imagined, great rivalry existed amongst the builders and owners, a rivalry which found expression in closely fought sailing matches held during the annual regattas which took place all round the area. The fishing boats were divided into four classes – those between 23 and 27 ft. were the largest, while the smallest group was of craft under 17 ft. Races started with the craft at anchor and sails lowered, waiting for the starting gun.

The opportunity to purchase boats no longer in work and to convert them to yachts was taken long before the contemporary enthusiasm for reviving old craft began. Their easily adapted hull and simplicity of maintenance made them particularly popular. One which is sailed in all her old style is the centenarian *Fanny,* launched at Cowes in 1872, was used largely for prawning and also for carrying oysters to market from Newtown, Isle of Wight. She is now a yacht on the East Coast.

Fishing vessels at Poole had many resemblances to the Solent smacks; they, too, lay at moorings and trawled and dredged for oysters, but had a rather heavier, fuller hull than their Solent equivalent. Unusually for work-boats, they were later fitted with centreboards, after about 1906.

The Cowes Ketch

One of the earliest representations of the modern version of the ketch rig is to be found in E. W. Cooke's masterly collection of engravings, published in 1829 and entitled 'Shipping and Craft'. Plate 40 is entitled 'A Cowes Boat' and it is what later became known as a Cowes ketch. These were the cargo-carriers of Spithead, Southampton Water and the Solent, linking the Isle of Wight with the mainland; humble craft and scarcely stout enough to venture beyond these sheltered waters. They were part of a world composed of voyages made on one, or at the most two, tides; they acted as sea-going carriers' carts loading cargoes of barrelled beer, bagged flour, iron chaff-cutters and mangles. Most of them sailed from Cowes and Newport, trading to the mainland. One, the *Bee,* round sterned like the vessel shown in 'Shipping and Craft', bridged the distance between the time of E. W. Cooke and our own. She was launched in 1801 at East Cowes by Hansen and lasted until 1926.

The Cowes ketch was carvel-built, double-ended and the earlier examples were constructed with the timberheads emerging through the covering board at the bow and stern and capped by a rail. Only later were bulwarks, about two feet high, of the normal type added. The deck-line had little sheer and a single large hatch amidship; they loaded some 30 to 40 tons on a shallow draught. The jib was set from a traveller on a short horizontal

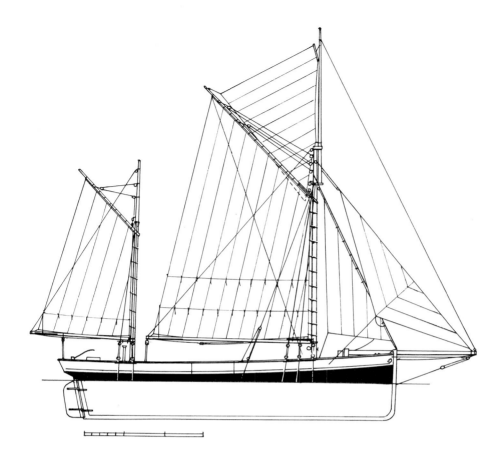

bowsprit that could be run in as was done aboard a fishing smack. The mizzen mast was stepped well aft, was unusually short, and both the mizzen and main gaffs were proportionately abnormally long in relation to their respective booms.

Cowes ketches were built by Hansen of East Cowes and White of West Cowes on the Medina river. The later ones had short square counters. They were amongst a wide range of craft employed on the coast and in the estuaries between Poole and Selsey Bill. Cement was manufactured on the Isle of Wight and elsewhere while Redbridge, above Southampton, had an industrial trade and sand and ballast were required for constructional work everywhere. Numerous waterside mills received their grain by barge. This kept a number of small boomie barges, fitted with lee boards, loading about 50 tons working from ports between Fareham to Poole while there was a group of sharp-sterned, pole-masted little traders that worked from Langston Harbour and had once worked on the Chichester Canal. A number of spritsail barges, identical to those found on the Thames were built locally and owned by the cement works while there were always mulie and ketch barges from the East Coast loading and unloading cargoes in the area. One of the strangest groups to be found there was a fleet of Norfolk wherries which had made a coastwise emigration from East Anglia and sailed cargoes of building materials within the confined waters of Portsmouth Harbour.

All these are now gone; only a few gaunt hulks lie in the mud as the tide ebbs and flows over Langston Harbour or mark the channel's edge which led to quays now only sought out by yachts and dinghys. The *Arrow*, last of the Cowes ketches, finished trading in 1938.

The Hastings Lugger

The Hastings boats so familiar to generations of visitors to the South Coast, were of three types. The largest were termed luggers; those slightly lighter and also decked were 'bogs', while the smallest, known as punts, were open beach boats. The luggers were between 27 to 30 ft. on the keel and built with full lines to enable them to be beached with as little danger as possible. Forward the lines were particularly full to give them plenty of buoyancy, and they were built as heavily as was compatible to their having to be hauled up the beach by capstans and then launched again over greased skids. The largest luggers had a displacement of between 7 and 16 tons while the smaller bogs had a tonnage between four and seven tons. The smaller punts were usually about 15 ft. overall and had only a small fore-deck.

The luggers were fitted with substantial bilge-keels. The use of iron centre-boards is exceptional amongst working craft in Britain but these were fitted to the luggers at Hastings, replacing the earlier use of lee-boards which must have been a sore trial when drift-net fishing. With the introduction of motors the centre-boards were discarded for the days of working to windward were over; only the smaller punts retained them. Before the

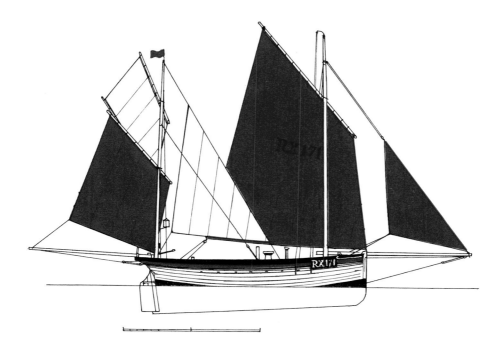

advent of the motor a full suit of sails was carried. It consisted of a big lug on the foremast supplemented by a mizzen lug with a yard topsail above it, a jib, mizzen staysail and occasionally a fore topsail. Trawling, drift-netting and long-lining were all undertaken although in the days of sail more trawling was left to the ketches sailing from Ramsgate and Rye.

The sterns of the luggers varied enormously; it gave them an individuality. Originally a vertical transom, it was extended by an overhanging projection, curving outward from the old transom. This form was termed a lute stern, but at the turn of the century an elliptical stern was introduced. The oak strakes of the hull were brought up from the quarters in a curving direction until each met its opposite number along the centre line; it did not lift so well in a following sea as the older lute stern. Variants of this elliptical stern, designed to obtain the best of the old and the new, were common.

A crew of six men and boys was carried in the days of sail and there was accommodation provided for them in the 'fore-room', with a stove set against the bulkhead; amidships was the space for nets called the 'chay'. Ballast was stowed on the ceiling amidships and in pre-motor days a wooden capstan was mounted aft of the main mast and worked by two men turning a crank on each side. When hauling the drift-nets a long pole was lashed for-and-aft between the main mast and the warp post amidships. Over this the nets passed and were shaken to clear them of fish, the catch finding its way below through the scud-holes, small apertures which were cut in the deck and could be securely sealed with blocks of wood.

Beaching a heavy fishing boat was made easier at Hastings by the employment of a horse-drawn capstan. Hauling off had to be resorted to at low tide and for this an anchor was dropped before beaching and the capstan on deck was manned by two men and the lugger dragged seaward over greased boards called 'trows'. The remainder of the crew scrambled aboard as the lugger became water-borne, using the chocks of wood provided on the stem to secure a foothold.

The Rye Trawler

There were a number of trawling bases in the days of sail which while they could not count their fleets in the numbers that were commonplace at such ports as Grimsby or Yarmouth, nevertheless had vigorous groups of smacks working from them. They fished the less easily trawled grounds which did not immediately attract the steam fishing boats. Rye Bay was one of these and at the ancient port of Rye were registered as many as 29 trawlers in the last quarter of the nineteenth century and as late as 1906 33 were based there. They fished during the winter months on the Diamond Bank, a ground abreast of Dungeness, and in Rye bay itself in the summer months, where the shallow water, only three to six fathoms, produced ugly conditions in winter and made trawling too unpleasant.

Rye smacks tended to be smaller and drew less water, for the harbour could only be entered with safety for an hour and a half before and after high tide. It was, no doubt, one of the factors that discouraged the introduction of steam-trawling. Rye boats landed their catches at Ramsgate, where there was also a respectable fleet of smacks before the First World War. Many of the Rye smacks were built on the banks of the Rother by two firms, Hoad and G. T. Smith. Both firms had built deepwater sailing vessels and the barges and smacks they built in the nineteen hundreds were the last of a distinguished line. G. T. Smith was responsible for launching smacks for all the major fishing ports from Brixham to Shields and their workmanship was of the highest standard. The hulls were disting-

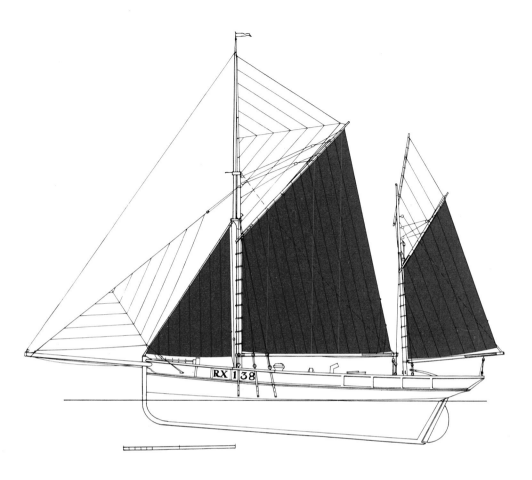

uished by a construction which set the frames in pairs and of single timbers with the points between the sections of the frames dowel-jointed. Some of the Rye smacks had been built by Smith in the seventies as cutters and then sawn in half and then had a section built in amidships. They were then rigged as 'dandies', as the ketch-rig was known. All had a square transom stern and had their bowsprits set to port of the stemhead. This was done as well as also leading the trawl warp through rollers to port to take account of the prevailing south-westerly winds and the trawling was done on that quarter. This allowed the smack to keep her bows to seaward when fishing and working towards the shore. Much of the fishing ground adjacent to Rye was the spawning ground for prime fish; special nets were used by the trawlers to ensure that small fish were able to escape the trawl's mesh. The Rye smacks fitted a steam capstan of the type which had an engine on the top and steam led to the piston by way of the hollow capstan spindle. It was used for hauling the trawl but also for setting sail and for all anchor work. The Rye smacks carried a shortened topmast in winter and jib-headed topsail. In summer a topmast at least ten feet longer was shipped and a big yard topsail was carried on the mizzen. G. and T. Smith were still launching fine wooden sailing trawlers until the nineteen twenties. The last one owned at Rye was the *Three Brothers*, built by them in 1896 and still fishing from the port 40 years later.

The Deal Lugger

The sloping shingle beaches in front of the Borough of Deal, the adjoining town of Walmer and close-by village of Kingsdown were once almost completely occupied by boats of differing sizes. Prince of these was the Deal lugger and it dominated the shores of the Downs throughout the second half of the nineteenth century. Deal lies opposite the channel and roadstead known as the Downs, while beyond are the nine miles of deadly sands, the Goodwins, which even today claim shipping. The eight to ten fathoms of water in the Downs made it a favourite place for ships to lie at anchor in the days of sail, sheltered by the mainland from south-westerly gales and to some extent by the Goodwins themselves. But the huge fleets of ships, numbering hundreds, that were attracted by the anchorage could find themselves plunging hawser-holes under and surging wildly as the gale mounted and the wind changed. Cables parted and damage, or worse, resulted. The luggers cruised the area and provided extra hands to vessels in need, took out supplies and ground-tackle to ships that required assistance, while occasionally they cruised down-channel putting pilots aboard homeward-bound ships.

The first-class lugger, for all its size and some were nearly 40 ft. long, was a great

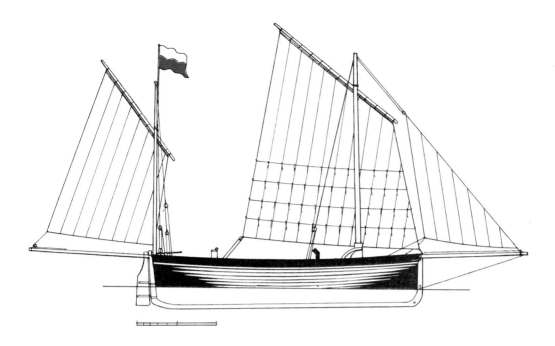

clench-built open boat. A decked fore-peak contained bunks and a stove to enable her crew of six to cruise for a week or more. The thwarts only gave transverse strength to the hull and when the men rowed they stood on the bottom boards and pushed, not pulled, the sweeps. Two large curved skegs supported the mast-case and guided the mast when it was lowered; all luggers carried a substantial wooden pump stepped forward of the thwart nearest the stern. A transom stern and straight stem was characteristic of all Deal beach-boats and the first-class luggers all had bilge keels and a fairly deep iron-shod keel. There was an eye in the fore and after end of the keel for securing the capstan cable when the luggers were returned through the surf.

The luggers were hauled up to their station at the top of the beach by heavy wooden capstans. The boats travelled over greased skids and then stood, bows facing the sea, their cables fitted with a quick-release hook, ready to plunge down the beach. At low-water hauling off warps had to be employed; these were lines anchored well out for the crews to haul in and so propel their luggers through the breakers.

The lugger's hulls were built with some twenty narrow varnished planks each side topped with a wide black-painted gunwale. The clench construction produced a light hull, easy to haul out and at the same time provided a buoyant shell of immense strength into which several anchors, each weighing a ton or more, could be loaded. The anchors were dredged from the seabed by the luggers in summer time and when required brought to the beach by a horse-drawn trug, man-handled aboard and then lashed down for the voyage out.

The luggers were two-masted, setting a lug foresail and mizzen; a jib was set on a traveller in fine weather. In the first-class luggers two foresails were carried and when going about the foresail was dropped, unhitched from the traveller on the mast and another hoisted on the other side as the lugger paid off on the new tack. The last of the first-class luggers, the *Cosmopolite,* was presented to Deal as a memorial to her kind, but unfortunately she was allowed to fall to pieces in the years following the First World War.

The Deal Galley

The first-class luggers were the largest of the five different types of open beach-boat that once lay cheek by jowl on the shelving beach facing the Downs. The smallest were the galleys and they outlasted the bigger craft by many years. Their smaller, lighter hulls required less maintenance. They even survived when the passing of the great fleets of sailing ships left only a handful of coasting-barges and schooners occasionally sheltering in the Downs and the purpose for which the luggers were built had gone. The galley-punts were rapidly equipped with engines as soon as they became available, but the more lightly constructed galleys were unsuitable for this adaptation and so remained the last reminder of the great days of the Deal boatmen.

They were long, clencher-built open boats, some 30 ft. overall, with a 5 ft. beam and less than three feet from gunwale to keel. The galley was designed primarily for speed in fine weather, for carrying out messages or ferrying passengers to ships, for taking out officials or a doctor to a vessel passing through the Downs and flying the appropriate signal. It is certain that they and their larger, similarly proportioned predecessors, which pulled six or seven oars, were employed in smuggling. They were light enough to be hauled over the Goodwin Sands to evade capture.

The keels of the galleys were of Canadian elm and the planking of the English variety,

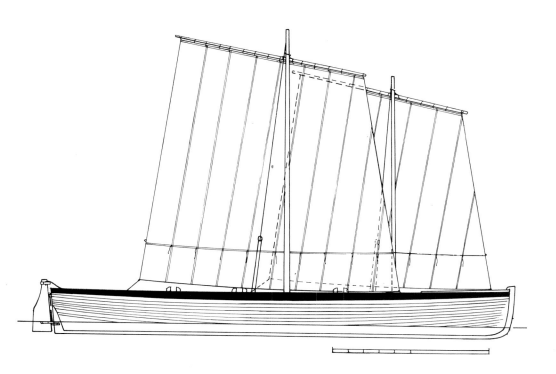

seasoned for one year only and between ½ in. and ¾ in. in thickness. Ribs of steamed ash were brought from Faversham, roughly formed to shape around moulds and then finished by the Deal and Walmer boat-builders. All the work-boats at Deal were varnished, never painted. The varnish not only set off the fine quality of the elm and oak planks but showed to all that cared to see that there was no disguising inferior wood or workmanship with putty or paint.

The galleys were planked with narrow elm planks, at least ten a side, fitted with five or six thwarts and light bottom boards with a grating fore and aft. They pulled five oars, one man at each and the helmsman steered with lines connected to a yoke over the rudder-head for the transom stern was very narrow. A small removable, watertight locker fitted under the centre thwart for 'vittles' and documents. Besides rowing, the galleys sailed. The centre thwart was fitted with a mast-case on its after side and a mast carrying an almost square-cut dipping lug was set. There was no rigging except for the yard halliard and downhaul, set up to weather, to a thumb cleat on the gunwale. Shingle ballast was carried aboard in bags and jettisoned before landing. Each boat was equipped with two masts. One was for use in summer with an appropriately proportioned sail. The summer mast was approximately 20 ft. in length while another was for setting a sail about two-thirds the size and was 16 ft. overall; both sails were provided with two rows of reef-points. Another mast-step, forward of the first thwart and fitted with an iron latch, was employed to step a 'norman post', a short timber upright to which a coir rope could be secured when towing astern of a steamer. This was used for stepping the shorter mast when during a calm, or competing in a regatta, both sails were set. As late as 1938 six galleys, most of them at least forty years old, competed in the Deal Regatta, all entered by representatives of families who had once owned first-class luggers and whose names were to be numbered amongst the heroes of the Goodwins.

The Whitstable Oyster Yawl

The smacks engaged in the Kentish oyster fishery at Whitstable, although cutter-rigged, were always known as yawls. It is inevitable that they should be compared with the Essex smacks employed in the same occupation. But to make such a comparison is a little unfair for the Whitstable boats did not tie up to moorings in the sheltered waters of muddy creeks at the end of a day's dredging, but had to find an anchorage offshore at Whitstable, open to the north. They were therefore more heavily built, with a fuller bilge and less draught than their equivalents on the opposite shores of the estuary. Few Whitstable yawls ever sought refuge in the harbour and some of the grounds where the yawls worked were only accessible by shallow draught boats.

The yawls worked the oyster beds offshore and were either owned or employed by the company that held the legal right to dredge them. Over one hundred yawls were employed by the company in the mid-nineteenth century, most of them relatively small, plump clench-built craft. The grounds were jealously guarded by watch-boats, themselves yawls, to see that no interlopers came to dredge. Colchester-registered craft would

occasionally come to the Kentish shore to seek brood (immature oysters) and deliver the catch to Whitstable where they were put down to grow to saleable dimensions. While, of course, oysters must only be eaten when there is an 'r' in the month, yawls were kept busy most of the year in an attempt to keep the grounds clear by dredging mussels and five-fingers and separating large oysters from small. This process went on except for the months of June and July, when the 'spat' fall is not to be disturbed, for this will ensure a good yield in years to come. It has been said that the yawls really cultivated farms under the water and there was no end to the work that was entailed to ensure a successful crop.

Carvel-built yawls, many built by Perkins at Whitstable, were introduced in the 'seventies and gradually replaced the older, smaller clinker-built boats. The new ones were 32 ft. on the keel and stoutly built of oak and elm. Each yawl worked up to five or six dredges: the largest was the ketch *Speedwell,* originally built for pleasure trippers at Herne Bay, and she was exceptional. A good yawl was designed to work across the tide, slowly dragging the iron oyster dredges, with their twine netting secured to the frame with hide lacings, covering as much ground as possible. As the smack worked back over the beds the oystermen sorted the haul, cleaning the oysters and placing them in baskets. There were still 80 yawls at work in the nineteen hundreds.

The yawls had minor differences: some had white-painted quarter-boards, some were copper-sheathed beneath the water-line to withstand infestation by marine-worm as they lay on the shore. Some were built with elliptical sterns, others with a square counter; all were fitted with a heavy barrel windlass in the bows and large freeing-ports along the rails to allow the decks to be easily cleared of the rubbish that accumulated when they were dredging. Some smacks went trawling and shrimping in the Thames estuary in summer and others voyaged far afield collecting oysters from distant layings.

Today the oyster grounds are but a shadow of their former glory and the yawls have gone. Dredging is done by motor-boats, dredging over the stern. A number of the yawls have been restored by enthusiasts and re-rigged in the authentic way with tall topmasts and immense bowsprits.

The Sailing and Pulling Lifeboats

The very first lifeboats, which were built in the eighteen hundreds, were designed primarily for propulsion by oars. Originating on the North-East coast where disasters occurred within almost hailing distance of the shore, fitting sails to the lifeboats was hardly necessary, for the distance to the vessel in distress could be covered by rowing. Above all, a lifeboat had to survive heavy breaking seas and, if possible, to right itself when capsized. The sailing lifeboat only developed as the efforts of the Movement widened and stations were built on coasts where there were offshore sands that brought vessels to grief far from the shore. Individual lifeboats varied from one station to another so that it is not easy to illustrate what may claim to be typical boats. But on the East Coast the Norfolk and Suffolk class evolved as a distinct type (upper drawing). Although, as were the others elsewhere, it was a type built in a variety of sizes. They owed much to the work of G. L. Watson, consultant naval architect to the Institution after 1881. The Norfolk and Suffolk class were all extremely heavy and built with a substantial iron keel and were between 34 and 46 ft. in length. It had long been apparent that there was an inevitable clash between the opposing characteristics of an unsinkable self-righting boat and one that, whilst sacrificing some of these qualities, was stable and while still retaining a wide margin of safety could work well under sail. The lower drawing shows the extremely high 'end boxes' fore and aft which gave the Self-Righting type its characteristic profile. Unlike the Norfolk and Suffolk type their sailing capacity was limited and the sails were of a comparatively small area, virtually storm canvas and the lifeboats reached their objective by either rowing or towing behind a steam tug.

The East Coast longshoremen, who provided the crews, voted unanimously for the Norfolk and Suffolk type, for they had many similarities and may even be said to have evolved from their beach yawls. They had the same flat floors, shallow draught and clench-build while the powerful rig of a dipping lug foresail was similar. They had twin iron centreboards and a guardrail along the gunwale, while water ballast tanks were fitted and were filled after launching. Common to both types was the broad belting of cork which combined to give buoyancy and protection when coming alongside vessels in distress. A Norfolk and Suffolk sailing lifeboat was long stationed at Gorleston which has seen more launchings than any other lifeboat station in Britain.

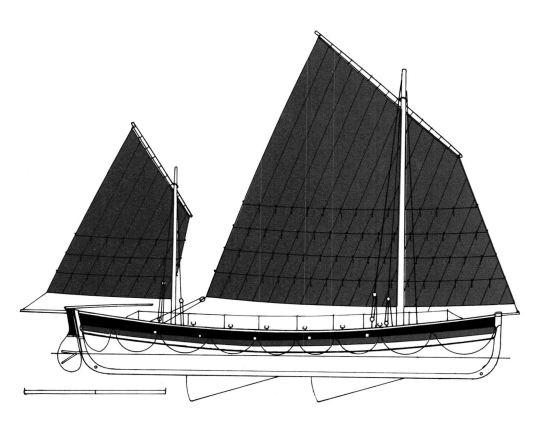

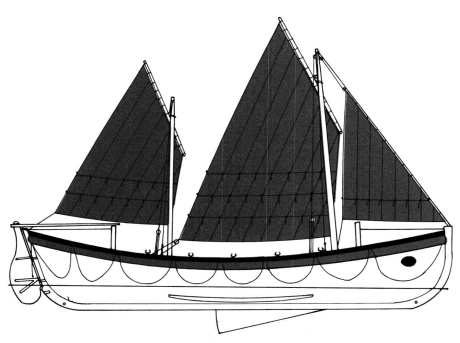

153

Glossary

Terms relating to parts of a vessel, fishing gear and rigging were often localised and showed considerable variation from port to port. There was no *lingua franca* that evolved as there was in the case of deepwater sail. However, most of those given here have a fairly general acceptance and refer to the meaning in the late nineteenth and early twentieth century.

Bilge The round in a vessel's timbers where they begin to approach the vertical. The part of the hull beneath the lining on either side of the keelson.

Bitts Substantial upright timbers which pass through the deck and mortice into the floors or keelson.

Brig Two-masted vessel, square-rigged on each mast and carrying a large fore and aft sail extended by a boom.

Bulkhead A transverse division of the hull.

Bumkin Iron bar extending from the stemhead, terminating in a hook to which is attached the tack of the foresail. (Bunkin, Cornwall).

Carvel Building a vessel in such a way that the planks are laid edge to edge and so present a smooth surface.

Clench Building a boat in such a way that the planks overlap, forming what are known as 'lands'; also known as clinker, clencher and lapstrake.

Coamings The raised edge to a hatchway; coamings could be important factors in providing longitudinal strength to a hull.

Counter That part of the hull projecting beyond the sternpost.

Cuddy The small area under the short foredeck of an otherwise open boat. (Cutty, Cornwall).

Dandy rig Originally a cutter rigged with a shortened main boom and a small mizzen. Later the term was used to indicate a vessel that would be better known as a ketch.

Demersal fish Bottom-feeding fish.

Fast An obstruction on the seabed encountered when trawling.

Floors The lowermost of those pieces which go to make up a frame, placed athwart the keel and into which it may be recessed.

Forecastle (Pronounced fo'c'sle). The area under the foredeck in the bows of a vessel; frequently used for the accommodation of the crew and stores.

Freeboard That part of a vessel's side above the waterline.

Gammon iron A circular band of iron fixed to the stemhead to accommodate the bowsprit.

Garboard The plank next to the keel and into which it is rabbeted and fastened.

Gasket A plaited cord fastened to the yard and used to secure a furled sail by wrapping it round.

Gooseneck A hook fitted to the mast end of a boom to secure to an eye on a snaffle round the mast and permitting it to move in any direction.

Gybe When running before the wind in a fore and aft rigged vessel to allow the sails to pass across the hull and to take up a position over the opposite quarter.

Halliard Any rope which is employed for hoisting a sail or yard.

Handspike A bar of wood used as a lever for rotating the barrel of a horizontal windlass.

Hank Detachable metal loop for securing a sail to a stay.

Hog piece A heavy piece of timber laid directly over the keelson and stretching nearly its full length.

Horse A wood beam, iron rod, chain or rope crossing the deck to which is attached the sheet of a sail in order to minimise the attention it requires when going about.

Hounds Those parts of a mast-head which project and are employed to support the shrouds. They are supported with wooden pieces called cheeks.

Jaws Wooden extensions to the inboard end of a gaff or boom, to allow it to rotate when attached to a mast.

Jibheaded A sail which has neither a yard nor a gaff at its head, but only a thimble to which the halliard is bent.

Keelson Timber lying on the floors, running above the keel and giving the vessel longitudinal strength. In the large Scottish luggers this was fitted below the floors.

Luff (n.) The weather edge of the sail. **(v.)** For a vessel to come up into the wind without completely losing way.

Lute stern A transom stern extended by knees and transversely boarded over for all or part of its length.

Moulding A fore and aft dimension.

Peak (n.) The upper corner of a fore and aft sail. **(v.)** To raise the peak of the sail as high as possible.

Pelagic fish Surface-swimming fish, usually found in shoals.

Ratlines Short lines worked across the shrouds at convenient intervals to provide a rope ladder for men going aloft.

Rockered Implies that a keel is considerably deeper at the stern than at the bow.

Scudding Clearing the herring nets over a pole above the fish hatch.

Sheer (n.) The longitudinal curve of a ship's side or deck.

Sheets Ropes by which a sail is controlled.

Siding A thwartship dimension.

Spinnaker A light sail when running before the wind, or a spritsail barge's jib topsail.

Spritsail A fore and aft sail where the peak of the sail is extended by a spar which crosses the sail diagonally and is secured at the foot of the mast.

Stemhead The top of the foremost upright timber in a vessel.

Tack (sail) The lower fore corner of a sail.

Thwarts Transverse seats in an open boat; referred to as thafts or thofts.

Ties A chain, rope or wire attached to a yard and passing through a sheave at the masthead with a tackle at its end.

Tommy Hunter Name given to a stay and purchase set up between the deck and the mizzen mast-head (East Anglian). A special rope strop used for raising the foremast (Cornish).

Topmast A mast fixed above the mainmast and secured to it; so arranged that it may easily be lowered to deck level.

Topsides The sides of the hull of a vessel between the rail and the curve of the bilge.

Transom (stern) A flat stern upon which the rudder is hung and beyond which there is no further projection of the hull.

Traveller An iron ring running freely on a mast or spar to which a sail is hooked prior to setting.

Trunking Taking fish from the smack to the fish carrier, also known as ferrying and boarding.

Weatherly Used to describe a vessel which will sail close to the wind and make little leeway.

Windlass bitts Stout upright timbers supporting the windlass in the bows of a vessel.

Bibliography

East Coast
COALS FROM NEWCASTLE R. Finch, Terence Dalton 1973
DOWN TOPSAIL H. Benham, Harrap (reprint) 1971
LAST STRONGHOLD OF SAIL H. Benham, Harrap 1947
ONCE UPÒN A TIDE H. Benham, Harrap (reprint) 1971
SAIL AND OAR E. Dade, Dent 1933
WHERRIES AND WATERWAYS R. Malster, Terence Dalton 1971

Scotland
FISHING BOATS AND FISHER FOLK ON THE EAST COAST OF SCOTLAND P. Anson,
    Harrap 1937
SCOTTISH SAIL, A FORGOTTEN ERA R Simper, David & Charles 1974

West Coast and Wales
BRITISH CORACLES AND IRISH CURRAGHS J. Hornell, Bernard Quaritch 1938
IMMORTAL SAIL H. Hughes, Robert Ross 1947

West Country
NO GALLANT SHIP M. Bouquet, Hollis & Carter 1959
WEST COUNTRY COASTING KETCHES W. Slade & B. Greenhill, Conway Maritime Press
    1974

South Coast
HEROES OF THE GOODWIN SANDS T. Treanor, The Religious Tract Society 1892
SOUTH EASTERN SAIL M. Bouquet, David & Charles

General
DEEP SEA FISHING AND FISHING BOATS E. W. Holdsworth, 1874
GAFF RIG J. Leather, Adlard Coles 1970
INSHORE FISHING CRAFT OF BRITAIN VOLUMES I AND II E. J. March, David & Charles
    1970
OLD SEA WINGS, WAYS AND WORDS R. C. Leslie, Chapman & Hall 1894
SAILING BARGES F. Carr, Conway Maritime Press 1971
SAILING DRIFTERS E. J. March, David & Charles (reprint) 1971
SAILING TRAWLERS E. J. March, David & Charles (reprint) 1972

SHIPPING AND CRAFT, ENGRAVINGS BY E. W. COOKE Commentary by R. Finch, Mast-head (reprint) 1969

THE MERCHANT SCHOONERS VOLUMES I AND II B. Greenhill, 2nd edition, David & Charles 1968

VANISHING CRAFT F. Carr, Country Life 1934

Index